Mr
Mensh

Mr
Mensh
Michael Rosen

Smokestack Books
1 Lake Terrace, Grewelthorpe, Ripon HG4 3BU
e-mail: info@smokestack-books.co.uk
www.smokestack-books.co.uk

ISBN 9781916012196

Smokestack Books
is represented
by Inpress Ltd

Contents

Rats

I was on New Cross Gate station and
it was late, trains were being cancelled,
there weren't many of us waiting, some
people had given up, gone back upstairs
and looking for night buses, the lights from
Sainsbury's were being switched off, and
I noticed some rats, they were coming out
of a concrete ditch next to the platform
and on to the platform itself, people said
that's what happens when people chuck
their take-aways away, they end up in that
ditch and the rats feed off it, and soon there
were as many as ten or even twenty rats
all over Platform 5 and some of them were
bold enough to come right up to our feet
as if our shoes were good to eat, and then
this guy with coloured trousers standing next
to me said he was starving, and I said, me
too, though I'd just had a houmous wrap
from the Beirut and he was staring at the rats,
like he was jealous of them that they had
plenty to eat and still no train came, and
he groped inside his jacket and took out
a kind of toasting fork, a long spiky fork
thing and before anyone said anything he
speared one of the rats. The rest of us
looked a bit startled but covered it with shrugs
and smiles and then he knelt down and killed
it with a little penknife. He took a flattened
tin can thing out of another one of his pockets,
laid it down on the platform, filled it up with bits
of stuff that I couldn't quite make out in the dark,
but he lit it with a lighter and laid a kind of grille
over the top of it, and just as quickly and neatly
put the rat on top. He was roasting the rat

on platform 5 of New Cross Gate Station. The little group of us standing there were staring and there was one guy saying over and over again, 'I don't believe this...' And still no train came and you could smell the rat cooking. I was wondering why he hadn't skinned it before he put it on the grill but he had other plans because after a while, he used his fork to pull the rat off and he laid it down on a paper plate he had pulled out of another pocket and he started to skin it. Just then we heard the train coming and though I wanted to see whether he really was going to eat it I was pretty keen to get home, I had an early start in the morning and so I got on the train and as it pulled out, I thought I saw him, pick a bit of the rat up towards his mouth, but I can't say I'm 100% sure of it.

Flies

I know flies. I've camped with them.
I heard how they eat. A lot of them land
on things and put down their proboscis that
sits at the front of their heads. Some saliva
comes out and this starts to digest whatever
they're sitting on. Then they suck the stuff
that they've started to digest back up their
proboscis. You can feel that saliva moment
just after they land on your skin, slightly moist,
slightly cool. Then there are the biting ones, that we
call horse flies. Their proboscoes are like daggers.
They jab that into your skin and suck the
blood up through the dagger. I thought I had
all this figured. The flies that do the saliva thing
are the ones we call house flies and the
bigger house fly type are blue bottles. And there are
some shiny green ones that love horse shit.
And the horse flies come in medium and large,
the medium ones are nippy and when they
land on you, you can hardly feel it, until they
stab you with the dagger. The large ones are
like flying caterpillars, fleshy and angry, and
a bite from them is like being attacked by a
fork-prong. Once I saw one by a swimming
pool waiting to get my shoulder. I grabbed a
flip-flop and threw it and it hit it, first time. End
of horse-fly. I've tried a hundred times since
and never got one. That's it, I thought: house
flies and horse-flies. Then one day we were
sitting at a table and I felt something bite me
and I looked down and all I saw was a fly. But
that kind of fly doesn't bite. A house fly. Then
there was another. These little house flies
were biting me. I got one and when it fell off,
there was a little drop of blood on my leg. I

picked it up and looked closely: its proboscis
didn't have the little spongey saliva bit on the
end. It was pointed like a tiny needle. It was a
tiny horse fly disguised as a house fly. It didn't
say it was a horse fly. It just turned up acting
like it was any old house fly but then did the
horse fly thing in my leg. Not just one of them.
There were hundreds of them. And under the table.
Always under the table.

Drop

Wasps are dropping from the lights
in the ceiling of the kitchen. They have
forgotten flight. They fall as if they are
dead, but on the table or the floor they
crawl a little. Wasps dropping. No buzz.
Straight from the light, and down.
There is hardly a hole in the ceiling for
them to come through, but they struggle
and make it. Some crawl over the light
and their shadows loom across the room.
And then drop. Above the lights they
must be queuing. Waiting their turn to
come down. They must know it's necessary
for them to go, and there's no information
coming back to them to tell them that
it's just a drop. There isn't anything else
for them down here. Just the table or the
floor. It's no home down here. They're not
treated well. They get brushed out. Or
stood on. Even the crackle from under
a shoe doesn't put off the next ones
coming through. Another one drops.
And another. And there's a sound. If
there's a piece of paper on the table,
when it drops on to that, it's nearly a
tap or a clap. That could be a warning.
But it isn't. They're still coming.

Flies II

The flies had died. The ground was pretending
to be frosted over but not making that good a
job of it. We made little clouds as we walked.
The flies had died. We said it was autumn. A
reasonable suggestion. But a decision was made
and summer came back. There was heat on my
back when I sat at the table. And by midday the
flies rose from the dead. Buzzing at the window,
hopeful that something nearby would be rotting.
Perhaps it was.

Pigeon

You pigeon, so grand, in your well-fed
suit walking our bit of grass like it's
the lawn at Downton Abbey, the one
you hire locals to mow. Little would
we know, you were the one who
drove straight at the bedroom window
smashed it and brought terror to
two seven year olds. It was you,
then, who couldn't get out, and
you couldn't make up whether to
walk or fly, every time you opened
your wings you hit the wall. And you
shat on the table. Not so grand. Then.
I opened the window and flapped
a towel behind you and you were away,
beating the air like nothing had happened.
Gone, without a thank you.

Tony

In his last days, Tony the cat became
more discerning and decided that
outside was not worth bothering about
and his litter tray was not up to scratch.
He found more amenable sites where
he could remind us that he was
still alive: the fire place, under the pipes,
behind the stove. It may have been his
version of the treasure hunt where
the only clue is the smell. And perhaps
he knew that we have lost some of
our powers of tracking scents and that
we would end up in the wrong corner of
a room, puzzled. But then, after a whole
morning looking, we'd find it, hurrahs all
round, a brief discussion over who had
stewardship of the treasure itself and
then the wait for the next hunt. Small
wonder he's much missed.

Round

I'm eating a round tomato.
I know it's round
because it came in a packet
that said 'Round tomatoes'.

The 43 Bus

On the bus indicator
It says the 43 bus is 'due'.
It doesn't come.
Then it stops saying
The 43 bus is due.
Where did the 43 bus go?
And where is the 43 bus now?

Real

A child in a school said to me,
'Are you real?'
I said yes.
He moved away,
came back and said,
'Really? Are you real?'
I got out my Goldsmiths college, ID card.
He looked at it and said,
'OK.'

Dentist

At the dentists today he sang Randy Newman's
Short People, he did the German tongue-twister:
'*Brautkleid bleibt Brautkleid und
Blaukraut bleibt Blaukraut*'
told me that he was friends with Meryl Streep's
double – who was Maltese and who was in
some kind of trick that the *Daily Mail*
played on the *Sunday Times* where
the *Sunday Times* thought they were
interviewing Meryl Streep but they weren't
and just the other day he met Cat Stevens'
brother in a cafe who was with the bloke
who played Romeo in the Zeffirelli film.
I said that I had had a dream about Meryl
Streep when I said to her that she was really
good in that film where she was in a raft going
over the rapids with Sam Neill and she said
thanks. He told me not to chew on the crown
for 24 hours because the glue is in the second phase.

Dentist II

I went to the dentist and he said that
I needed a filling, a huge filling, massive,
really, really big. I said OK and he gave
me an injection and while we waited for
it to take effect he said what music would
I like on, you can have classical, pop, jazz,
whatever you like and I said, jazz please
and he said that he was writing a novel,
it's about this Jewish kid who was
adopted by the Pope and I could feel the
injection spreading through my jaw like a
finger in my gum and there was Miles Davis
doing *So What* on the speaker and that gave
me such a good feeling of sitting in my old friend
Dave's room and Dave saying that this is the
greatest record ever made, and me thinking
how does Dave know that, how can he be so
certain and to think – hah! – it wasn't all that long
after it came out and in a way, Dave was right
and he was – what? – only sixteen at the time,
fancy being 16 and listening to that album, and
knowing that it was great and the dentist said
Spielberg was on to the story and was making a
movie about it but Spielberg was basing it on a
history book he'd got hold of not his novel and
I said how I wrote a book about a kid who spends
the night at a museum long before the *Night in the
Museum* movie came out and he said that the
filling was going to be enormous, huge, massive,
and he got cracking and I closed my eyes and
concentrated on flattening my back out in
the chair and breathing and he said to the
assistant, 'Wedge', and I wondered what that
could be, and then I heard the drill – such a
high pitch – and he said to the assistant,

'Come over here, take a look at this,' and she
went around to his side, and looked in and I
could hear her take in a sudden breath, and
he said, I've never seen that before, and she
said, 'Neither have I,' and I said, 'What?' though
really it was just a kind of questioning grunt
because I had the suction thing in on one side
that was hauling all my spit out and somewhere
in there was the thing he called the wedge, and
he said, 'Well, I think I can see your brain.' And I
said, 'What colour?' but I think he thought I said,
'Fuck off' because he said, 'No. I mean really.' So
I tried to ask him, 'What was he going to do about
it?' And because I couldn't say it properly, I did
a kind of shrug meaning, what to do? And I meant
it quite urgently because I didn't really want my brain
exposed like that, I don't know much about brains but
I was pretty sure that a brain shouldn't just be hanging
out in the middle of a dentist's surgery. But I think he
took the shrug as a kind of Jewish shrug, meaning,
'Hey, so! It's no big deal, there are worse
things in life than a bit of brain being on show.'
So, he said, 'Too right, I like the attitude. Do you
mind if I take a picture of it?' And I did a gesture
meaning, 'You go ahead,' and he got that gesture
OK and put his phone right next to my mouth and
he said, 'Got it, thanks. I won't put it up on social
media or anything,' and I gave him a thumbs up
because actually I was quite grateful that people
would not be tweeting pictures of my tooth with
this – like – tunnel leading up to my brain because
next thing I'd be on a station somewhere
and someone would come up to me and say,
'Sheesh, saw your brain on Facebook, man,'
and he showed the pic to the assistant and she
said, 'That's good,' and in a way I felt kinda
flattered that she thought my brain looked good
but then I thought O maybe she just means that

her boss has taken a good picture and – hey –
who knows, there might be some whole thing
about her having to say that his photos were
good because of whether she got a bonus or not
and he said, that he needed to 'pack' the whole
now and because it led up to my brain, it might
start affecting how I thought with that part of
the brain, and I said, 'What part of the brain
is it?' And he said, 'It's the part of the brain
that deals with chickens.' And I said, 'Will it mean
that I won't be able to see or hear chickens, is it that?'
And he said that he wasn't sure because people
react in different ways to having packing put in
right close to the brain. And I said but you said that
you had never seen anything like this before, it
sounds like you have seen a few people with this
tunnel up to the chicken-part of the brain and he said,
who's the dentist here? And I pointed to him. I very
carefully pointed at him with one finger so that he was
in no doubt that I thought that he was the
dentist here. And I think he took that pretty well.

Hi!

'Hi, we've noticed that you've been listening
to a lot of radio and watching a lot of TV recently.
Good choice! But guess what, from now on, you
don't have to. Our trained listeners and viewers
can do it for you. It's simple, it's cheap,
it's convenient. This is how it works:
You get up in the morning, and if you're anything
like the rest of us, your head feels heavy, you're
dying for that coffee, you can't bear the sound of
anything buzzing in your ear. One thing you
really don't want is to hear radio. What we do
is send someone over to your house and we
take your radio into another room, switch it on
and listen for you. Then, when it's time for you
to move on to your other tasks – whatever they
are – we just leave. It's as simple and as easy
as that. Again, come evening, maybe you think
you've got to switch on that radio, watch that TV
sitting in the corner of your living room. No!
Not anymore. We can do it for you. Yes, round we
come, and do the job. You can go off and do
anything you like, and you have absolute peace
of mind that someone is listening to your radio and
watching your TV. And – here's the coolest part –
we don't tell you anything at all about what's been
on! Imagine that! You will have no idea at all what
all that radio and TV has been going on about.
And we're not just one-shot jonnies. This is a
24-hour service, our listeners and viewers
will be with you within minutes.

C'mon. Give us a try. You know you want to.'

Deleted

It took me some time to discover that some
emails intended for me sometimes arrive
straight into a folder called 'Deleted'. I
hadn't deleted them. They contain
important information. Stuff that I need.
Like where I've got to be. And when. And
yet they're in 'Deleted'. Who decided that
I shouldn't know where I should be? And
when? For some time people had been saying
to me, 'I sent you the information the other
day.' And I would say, 'No, it didn't come in.'
And we would say, 'Hah! Email, eh?' like
these emails had disappeared into a space
we couldn't describe, a dimension that doesn't
exist a square-root-of-minus-one dimensions
or, there is a vacuum cleaner in California that
hoovers up emails. 'Hah! Cyberspace!' we said,
like we were saying something that had any
meaning. And then, I don't know why, one day
I peeped into this place called 'Deleted' (if it is
a place) and there was an email full of
information about where I was supposed
to be. It was hard not to feel for a moment that
a hidden hand had intervened in my life, saying:
'Hey you, I don't want you to read this!' But then,
I thought it was kinda worse to think of it as odder
than that: machines randomly ranging across
humankind, deleting millions of messages under
the pretence of doing us a favour. Like even at
the moment of creating instant worldwide
conversations, it prevents them happening too.
And I thought how yesterday I forgot a thing that
I had only just remembered. It was as if I had
sent it from one part of my brain to the other
and then deleted it without asking for my permission.
But, hey, at least I did that. I think.

File

The file you have been working on for the
last hour is going to crash. We are going to
quit. This computer is going to do that thing
where your screen is going to revert to that
naff image you've got on your desktop. The
file that you were working on will stop existing.
It won't be anywhere. There is a button called
'diagonistics' which you can press, wait for about
three weeks and get a message which will say
that an error called something like DF110 (which
is in fact a painkiller) has just happened. This
implies it is your fault that the file has
disappeared. Usually we find that the files that
disappear are ones that punters like you have
grown overly attached to. Perhaps it was a story
or a poem or an article. You were probably
getting locked in, fully engaged with what you
were trying to say, getting that satisfaction where
the words felt right, the phrasing had a kind of
rhythm and the ideas seemed to flow from one
part of the file to another. We expect there
were one or two jokes in there that you had just
made up. OK, not exactly jokes, perhaps more
like wry comments, or that thing where you
repeat things but in different ways for effect.
The weird thing is, we could lay money on it,
you've probably forgotten the best bits. That'll
be because they were so new. And extra-weird
that you had only just made them up, so surely
they were right at the front of your brain so
for goodness sake they should be still there.
But they're not. Gone. You'll notice that we've
used the word 'unexpectedly' before the word
'quit' which is not strictly true. It's not 'unexpected'
for us. We do it all the time. We roam

round the world unexpectedly quitting all over the place. Wherever we see a computer that's been running along in a fine and dandy way, we hurl in an 'unexpectedly quit'. Have a nice day.

Tudors

I was doing a history exam on the Tudors and
Stuarts and there was a question on whether
the Justices of the Peace in Tudor times were
central to how the Tudors maintained power
and while I was busy answering it, I glanced
down at the exam paper and there was a
question I hadn't noticed. It said, 'If you had
to choose between three different types of
toothpaste what would be the criteria you would
use to determine your choice?' Then it had
some qualities of toothpaste and you had to
tick in whichever boxes mattered to you the
most. There was: 'the toothpaste claimed that
it would whiten your teeth'; 'the toothpaste
claimed to freshen up your mouth'; 'the
toothpaste would help your gums stay healthy'
and 'the toothpaste would help you see in the
dark'. I ticked the one about the toothpaste
helping me see in the dark because I thought
that would be very useful, particularly some time
when I was in the bathroom and the light's not
working, not even in the little glass wall cabinet
where I keep my nail scissors and indigestion
pills, not that I've had indigestion for some years now.

Raspberry Pip

All hail to the raspberry pip, survivor, desperate to
stick between the teeth; wedge itself like a pebble in
a tyre-tread; it refuses to be dissolved or shrunk,
it hunkers down, cornered, resisting a poking with
your finger-nail, and even the tooth-pick can fail.

All hail to the raspberry pip, hiding in its scarlet globule,
migrating into your mouth, a bird's beak, a fox's jaw,
disguised as softness, waiting to be munched, ready
for the peristalsis, the long slide through.

All hail to the raspberry pip, heading for a spot of dirt, a
railway siding, where it becomes a bramble, winding and
arching its thorny way, obstreperous enough to delay
your longing for the fruit until it has fully scarletted.

Dogs

After dogs have weed on
ten lampposts
there's no more wee to wee
but they go on to the next lamppost,
lift a leg
and mime weeing.

A Sign

The mysterious sign
on a message
I was about to post
was not,
I discovered,
an emoji
that I had mistakenly added.
It was a fragment
of curried rice
from last night
that had attached itself
to my computer screen.

Helpful

I was being executed the other day.
Just as the axe was hovering over my neck,
a very nice journalist
stepped forward and removed a mosquito from my arm.
'You don't want to get stung,' he said
and the axe dropped and killed me.

Firing Squad

I was up before a firing squad once
and they said that before I died
I could read out something.

I said, Thank you.

And I started to read out
my copy of *King Lear*
that I carry with me
and by the time I got halfway through,
the regime was overthrown
and I was released.

Panettone

Never
Forget
To
Nibble
The
Remnants
Of
The
Panettone
Off
The
Paper.

Problem

The bumblebee
doesn't understand
glass.

Avoid

I had an egg and tomato sandwich
on a trip to Chessington Zoo
in 1955.
Since then I have avoided
egg and tomato sandwiches.

A Bad Day

I just sent myself
an email.
It came back as
undeliverable,
addressee not known.

Log in

'Log in using your email'
(I log in using my email)
'That email has already been taken'
Yes, by me, you binary buffoon.

Ancient

My body isn't now.

It's carrying ancient genetic information
of the past
and future.

My cells are coming into being
and dying in millions of
other chronologies.

For a moment
I thought my teeth
might be as old as me
but they are about
ten years younger.

The Hem and the Toe Nail

The design of the inside of the bottom of a trouser leg
seems to involve – more often than not – a hem...
which is good because this
prevents the bottom getting
frayed and no one wants a
frayed bottom
unless it's the style
which of course it has been with
plenty of trousers having frayed
bottoms.
However:
back with the hem.
If you put a hemmed trouser on
without wearing socks,
this brings your big toe nail into
direct contact with the hem.
Usually this results in a blockage,
jam or impasse as the toe nail
reaches the hem.
No matter how much you bend the toe
or the foot, or shake the trouser,
the blockage remains.
The only immediate way out of the problem
is to bend down and release the hem from the toe-nail.
Inevitably, the same will happen with the other
toe-nail and the trouser hem on that other leg.
The solution is, as I have suggested,
put on socks first.
There is a problem with this, though:
it does mean standing around for a few seconds
in your underpants and socks.
I'm not saying this looks ridiculous
but it possibly is.

The Wart and the Toe Nail

In 1961 a guy called Wilkinson stamped
on the big toe of my right foot and a few
months later the nail fell off. It had
turned several colours before the day it
worked itself loose: red, purple, yellow,
green. Sometimes combinations of all
four, like a sunset over a city, infused
with sulphur. I kept the nail. It was in the
same cardboard box as the name-tags my
mother sewed into my PE kit, the medal I
won for winning the Metropolitan Walking
Club's Novices Race, my father's US ARMY
brass brooches, the drawer from an East
German wooden money box, and a stone
from the bed of the River Monow. I took
the box with me to university and when I
moved into digs run by a Polish woman and her
cab-driving husband, it was there alongside
my Anglo-Saxon poetry books. By then it
was beginning to twist and had turned brown,
and on the surface that had been next to the
quick of my toe, there was a curd-like residue
of something organic. This may seem unrelated
but on my right hand I had several large warts.
They had appeared there as a result of holding
the hand of someone who had several large
warts on her left hand. I shared the digs with
John who liked to probe around in the cardboard
box and though he liked the drawer to the East
German money box and my father's US ARMY
brooches, he was sickened by the toe-nail. He
was critical of some side-whiskers that had
cropped up on my face and not at all keen on
the warts. He was highly skilled at doing the voices
of a sergeant-major reciting *Jabberwocky*, a

professor of Latin who translated and
recited the poems of Catullus that focussed
on fellatio, and Geordie women in a sausage
factory who had pulled down his trousers and
smothered his stotts in the jelly that was used
to make sausage skins. He was so good
at these voices that there were times he would
be doing the performance along with many others
long past midnight, at the very moment when I had
to be writing my essay on Anglo-Saxon poetry.
John wouldn't leave my room and we
would hear the cab-driving landlord coming
home and his Polish wife greeting him like he
was liberating her homeland – a kind woman,
though not keen on the fact that when we washed
up in the bathroom sink (not a frequent event and
there were no other sinks to wash up in), bits of
spaghetti bolognese lingered in the plug hole.
There was nothing I could say, either funny or
hostile that would move John to leave. One night
I put the toe-nail next to the largest wart – one that
looked like the cross-section of a cauliflower on the
fleshy part of my middle finger – and walked
towards him. The doubling up of the nail and
the wart was so unpleasant for him that he left
immediately. Last time I saw John, he was living
on his own in a ground floor flat on the Marylebone Road.

Parking

A text came through on my phone
telling me that my car was coming
to the end of its parking time and
did I want to extend the time it was parked?
Yes, I thought, I do? I would really like that.
There was a number and I called.
The recorded message asked me
the reg number of my car and I
tapped that in. The message then
asked me to tap in how many hours
I would like to add on. I tapped in 4.
The message said that this was an
invalid number. So I tapped in 6.
The message said that this was an
invalid number. So I tapped in 2 and
the message said, 'The call is ended.'
I thought that's a pity, I was just getting
to enjoy it. I found that I was strangely
attracted to the efficient but urgent tone
of the woman talking to me. I liked the
way that she seemed to be so good
at getting things done. And now this.
Out of the blue: the call is ended. I
wondered if it was something about
the way I tapped the keys. Was I a
bit clumsy? I know that I had just eaten
a sandwich and maybe she had picked
up the whiff of mayonnaise on one
of the numbers. And it wasn't as if
it was me who had been in touch
in the first place. She was the one
who had texted me. I figured that she
must sit there all day, day after day,
texting people telling them that they
can extend their hours and then snubbing
them with that 'The call is ended' thing.
Maybe that's what she's into. The snub.

Detail

A man read my book about me and wrote
'Sometimes there's too much detail in this
book and sometimes there isn't enough' and
I thought about the things in my life that are
very detailed, which I had mentioned like the
fact that I liked the sound of a blues harmonica,
being played over an electric guitar, so
maybe that was too detailed for him, or was it
the fact that a man called Jimmy looked out
at the lights in Hatch End station when he was
talking to me? That was also very detailed. And
then I thought about things where it wasn't
detailed. Would that have been that I hadn't
mentioned the colour of my brother's hair? Or
was it that I didn't describe the windows in my
secondary school? The more I thought about
these things, the more confused and worried
I got, thinking of the man reading my book,
saying as each page went by, 'Too detailed!'
and 'Not detailed enough!' and I imagined him
with a lover and the lover saying, 'Really? Oh
dear. How annoying. That is poor' because
lovers can be very supportive like that, particularly
when you're reading a book, though if you had
just had a row, you can imagine that a lover
might just act contrary and whenever he said,
'Oh god, not enough detail' the lover said, 'Well
isn't that you? Never satisfied with what you've
got. What do you want him to tell you, where he
was on the night of April 3rd 1954?'

And he would say, 'Why don't you respect my
judgement on things? Whenever I express an
opinion you jump down my throat like I don't
know what I'm talking about...' and it could all
get quite nasty very quickly.

Broom

I went to this shop that sold household goods
and I asked for a broom and the man said, we
don't sell brooms on Thursdays. Oh, I said,
that's a shame. He said, yes it is, would you
like a bin? No, I said, I've got a bin. He said,
you could have another bin, everyone needs
bins. That's true, I said, everyone does need
a bin. So much rubbish, he said. Yes, I said,
there is a lot of rubbish. And a lot of dirt. Yes,
he said, there is a lot of dirt and... that's why
I need a broom, I said. Yes, he said, I bet you do;
with so much dirt around everyone needs a
broom. Yes, I said. Yes, he said. I thought
I had made some progress so I said, And
there really is no chance of buying... No, he
said, not on Thursdays. And I said, was there
a special reason why he didn't sell brooms on
Thursdays and he said, no. He just didn't
want to sell brooms every day. So I said,
could he move his non-broom selling day
to another day this week, like Friday or Saturday
and he said, Friday is the day that he doesn't
sell bins and Saturday is the day he doesn't
sell tea towels and he didn't want to mess up
the timetable. I said, no, you don't want to mess
that up, you'd be all over the place... what about
Sunday? I said. What about Sunday? he said.
You know, I said, what don't you sell on Sunday?
What are you talking about? he said, why
would I not sell things on a Sunday? And I
said, no reason, no reason. And he said, so
you don't want the bin?
And I said, no, I don't want the bin.

Dog

One guy inherited a tiny plot of land and
there was an old vintage threshing machine
sitting on it, so he broke it up and burned it
and for a while he brought his kids over to
the plot and had picnics there but he seemed
to have got bored with that until one day
he came with a dog and put the dog on a lead,
tied the lead to a post and he leaves the dog
there now, all day and all night. Of course he
comes to feed it once a day but that's it,
and the dog is quiet some of the time but most
of the time it barks. It barks at birds and there
are magpies and pigeons and turtle doves and
buzzards coming over, it barks when it hears
other dogs which is quite a lot of the time
because a lot of the people around have dogs,
and it barks when it thinks there are mice or
rats or voles or snakes or wild boar or badgers
or foxes or deer and plenty of them are coming
through and it barks at owls and there are the
screech owls and the tawny owls and the little
owls all around and it barks if you make a noise
like 'Yeah, get in!' if you score a goal, and it barks
at motor bikes and it barks at fire engines and
ambulances and it barks at flies and wasps and
hornets and it barks at spiders and butterflies
and moths and bats and beetles and caterpillars
and ants and it barks when it hears a walnut or
hazelnut or an apple or a pear or a plum or an
acorn falling off a tree and it barks when it hears
itself barking.

Back

I went to the doctors and said I've
got a bad hip, my hip hurts. He said,
stand up. I stood up. He said, take
off your shirt. I took off my shirt. He
said, turn round. I turned round. It all
went quiet. I looked over my shoulder
at him. He was looking at my back.
It's bent, he said, it's curved. Is it? I
said. Yes, it's what we call scoliosis.
Right, I said, who did that? You did,
he said. I did? I said, when? I don't
remember curving my back. No, he
said, I don't suppose you do. What
did I do, I said, did I lean? Possibly, he
said. But from what you're saying, one bit
of me leant one way and another bit
of me leant the other? Yes, he said,
So have I got to lean back now? I said.
Yes, he said. How will I know when
I've leaned back enough? I mean, I don't
want to do a whole lot of leaning back
and discover that I've leaned too far,
otherwise I'll have to lean back again
the way I came from, I said. Good point,
he said, you don't want to lean too
much. Is that it then? I said. Do you
smoke? he said. No, I said. That's good, he said.

Camembert

I once went to a Camembert factory.
There were hundreds and hundreds
of Camemberts. What they did was
pour milk into Camembert
shaped collars. Then, as we walked
along, we walked from Camemberts
that had just been poured, to
Camemberts that had been there for
one week, two weeks, three weeks,
four weeks, on and on until it got
to ripe Camemberts. I was 13 and I
had never eaten Camembert. I thought
that they smelled of old socks and
there was no point in going round a
factory that was making old socks
out of milk but I was with my friends
Mart and Chris; and Mart said that he
loved Camembert and each time we
stopped and the man said, '*une
semaine*' (one week), or '*deux semaines*'
(two weeks) and so on, he gave Mart
some to taste and each time, Mart said,
'Mmmm, this is great,' and you could
see bits of the soft smelly milky stuff
on his lips and inside his mouth and I started
to feel sick but on we went, '*trois semaines*'
'Mmmm', '*quatre semaines*', 'Mmmm'
and it got smellier and smellier and the bits
of milky stuff on Mart's lips were getting stickier
and stickier and Mart licked his lips and you could
see his tongue was covered in the thicker slimier
stuff so that when it flicked out of his mouth
it put more creamy lumps on to his lips, though
it didn't really flick as it was so coated.

Every Valley

It wasn't that we were enthusiastically Christian.
In fact, we weren't Christian at all but my brother
who loved singing was in a choir that was going
to sing Handel's *Messiah*. And he practised at home.
From another part of the flat, we would hear,
'Every valley shall be exalted'.
It came into my head: 'Every va-alley'. And it was
going to be exalted. And the 'exalted' came out as
'exal... ted'. But which valleys? Where were
these valleys? We went on camping holidays
and walked up valleys. We camped in
a valley in Wales. Would it be exalted? And what
is exalting? How do you exalt a valley? I was 12
and I didn't have the answer to these questions
but because my parents started singing it round
our flat, 'Every valley shall be exalted' as well as
my brother, I didn't ask. It was just an obvious thing
that you could sing about. The valleys were going to
be exalted. And there were other bits that stuck too:
'All we like sheep who've gone astray-ay-ay-ay-ay...'
That was the valley in Wales again. The farmer had
hundreds of sheep and some of them went astray.
My mother thought this one was funny. I had no idea
why she thought that was funny. We might be
listening to the radio and some item on the news
would set her off singing, 'All we like sheep have
gone astray-ay-ay-ay...' And everyone would join in.
Me too.

Northumberland

He took me, a boy of eleven, up on the moor and showed me sheep
stuck on their backs. 'They roll over to scratch theirselves.
The wool takes up the water they can't rise.'
He grabs a blackface and heaves it out of the hollow.
'They die if I don't do that.
You and your mum and dad don't believe in God do you?'
He took me to the stable and showed me a cow
with a chain round her neck. 'Milk fever,' he says.
He holds a bottle above her neck, runs a tube down to a needle.
He jabs the needle into the cow. A big bubble swells up
under the cow's skin around the root of the needle.
Her eyes roll and whiten.
'You're afraid she'll die, aren't you? I'm not afraid of death.
You are.'
He took me into the field
and showed me a cow with her calf
lying in the pool of its afterbirth.
'If it doesn't get up
I'll have to take it away.
If I touch it too soon, mind
the cow won't have anything to do with it. Reject it.'
We watched.
'Could you kill a man?'
I had to choose. Kill or be killed.
What would you do?
'There it's up – it won't need a bottle. The cow'll eat all that stuff now.
You wouldn't, would you?'

The Pigman

The tide of war retreated across the suburbs
leaving gas-masks in attics, a man with one leg
on the bench by the library, an air-raid shelter
in the park which one day, the kid with the
most nerve took us down and where we found
beds and broken bottles and imagined a life of
riley back in the days just before we were born.
After all we could go to the Empire restaurant
that had survived the war too, along with talk of
doodlebugs and uncles who disappeared in
places I couldn't pronounce. The internet has
unearthed other leavings: piggeries. Sited, they
said on scrubland or in unused corners of parks
and I remembered how, amongst the nettles and
brambles, behind a fence made of old doors and
prams, in the air-raid shelter park, a red-faced man
in a dung-coloured coat, stood by a corrugated
stye, in the midst of stink. We called him the pig-man
and after our explorations in the dumps and streams
just as the lamplighter on his bike cycled round
pulling the lever with his pole and hook, so that
the gas mantles fizzed and lit, we hiked through
the nettles to get a look at the pig-man. We
cackled at him, as if he had no place in our park,
and this would rouse him to tell us to clear off out of it,
which made us cackle all the more till we hacked
our way out and left him with his pig, never
knowing that he had been part of the what our
teachers called the war-effort.

Lone Ranger

When I was a kid, we had no TV.
Just imagine that: no TV! How did
we live?! Then one day the TV arrived.
Two guys brought it in. It was huge.
Like a wardrobe. It was bigger than them.
They struggled to get it in through the door.
It was massive. Only the screen... was tiny.
It was about as big as a slice of bread.
And it wasn't colour. Do you know what it was?
No, not black and white. Black and white
hadn't been invented yet. It was grey and grey.
And you couldn't really see what was going
on. All that happened was there were smudges
moving across the screen. Some of them were
light grey. Some of them dark grey.
My favourite programme was *The Lone Ranger*.
There was a tune that went with it,
William Tell's Overture. We all learned how to sing it, going:
daddle an, daddle an
daddle an dan-dan,
daddle an, daddle an
daddle an dan-dan
daddle an daddle an
daddle an dan-dan
daddle aaaaaaan, dan-dan!
The Lone Ranger had a mask.
You could never see his eyes.
We used to make a mask with our fingers
so that we looked like the Lone Ranger.
At the beginning of every programme
a voice said: 'A fiery horse with the speed
of light, a cloud of dust and a hearty Hi-Yo Silverrrrrr!'

And a light grey smudge –
that was the Lone
Ranger's white horse –
went across the screen.
We all learned how to say: 'A fiery horse with the speed
of light, a cloud of dust and a hearty HiYo Silverrrrrr!'
Then in the programme, the Lone Ranger did all
sorts of good deeds but at the very end he would disappear.
No sign of him anywhere.
There would just be two people standing there
and one would turn to the other and say,
'Who was that man?'
And the other would say, 'That was... the Lone
Ranger.'
We all learned how to say that. We used to say it to
each other in school.
'Who was that man?'
'That was... the Lone Ranger!'
And then the music would come back:
daddle an, daddle an
daddle an dan-dan,
daddle an, daddle an
daddle an dan-dan
daddle an daddle an
daddle an dan-dan
daddle aaaaaaan, dan-dan!

That's how exciting things were in 1955.

Maria and Georg

Maria and Georg Kroshniewitz lived in a small flat
in North London with their three children. Ever since
she was a small girl, Maria had made small moving
toys. Using parts of old construction kit games, she
would make windmills and cranes and trucks. When
she first met Georg, she kept this skill secret, not
wanting him to know that she had this deep interest,
deep longing to make moving objects. He was
visiting her one time and while they were talking of
an old movie they had both seen, a sound
came from the cupboard behind them, a whirring
noise that stopped, started, and stopped again. It
sounded like a kettle beginning to boil. Curious,
Georg asked Maria and though she tried to laugh
it off, Georg persisted and in the end she opened the
cupboard and showed him dozens of automata.
He could hardly believe that Maria had made them
herself but it wasn't long before she showed him
just how she could and told him how she had spent
years at it. He was intrigued and then bit by bit
became obsessed with it himself. They became
a couple and had three children and all the while
they made their little automata, moving now on to
little robots and more lifelike forms that walked
and danced. And all the time it was something
private and domestic and their children grew up
amazed and delighted by them but ultimately
taking them for granted. It was what they all did,
invent, make and play with automata. One time
the middle child took one to school for an open
day and it so happened that one of the parents
who came, worked in television and it wasn't
long before Maria and Georg and the children
were showing their models and robots on a
TV show. In the modern way, one short sequence

from the show – where the robot danced beautifully
to a joyful samba song and then appeared to
slap the show's host, went viral. Maria and Georg
were in demand all over the world. I say, 'Maria
and Georg' because the children didn't want
to be part of it. No amount of pressure from
TV moguls, hosts of shows, and PR people would
convince them that they should take part in the
demonstrations and spectacles that were devised
by the TV companies. But, Maria and Georg pressed
on, using their old automata, making new ones,
devising new shows while the children, growing up
now into older teenagers, kept their distance. They
were supervised mostly by various au pairs, live-in
nannies, and cooks enabling Maria and Georg to tour
the world. The children had their own ambitions:
one wanted to be an archaeologist, one a jazz
guitarist and one an accountant. With their new-
found wealth, Maria and Georg created an
automata lab and started to push the technology
to its limits. Some of it was top secret as it
involved workmanship at a micro level. The point
of it all was the marriage between the old and
the new. And this was the charm. It was all a
fantastic success, until disaster struck and the
automata lab was burnt to the ground. At first it
was assumed that it was an accident. It had
a terrible effect on both Maria and Georg who
found that mentally and physically they couldn't
pick it up and start again. They began to argue
and fight and bit by bit they each started to
suspect that the other had been responsible for
the fire. They each started to find motives as to
why they might each have started it, Maria
accusing Georg of envy, Georg accusing Maria
of greed and resentment – both claiming that this
went back to the beginning of their relationship.
In the end, they couldn't bear each other's

company anymore and split. There was hardly any wealth left, because the automata lab company was over-capitalised and some kind of dodgy financing structure landed them in debt. At the same time, the child who wanted to be an archaeologist showed symptoms of a fatal illness. The separated parents were desperately obsessed with the whys and wherefores of their own destruction to be terribly concerned with their dying child. She eventually died at the age of 22 and following her death, the jazz guitarist child came to Georg and told him that the archaeologist had confessed that she had caused the automata lab to burn down. How was that possible, said Georg? And the guitarist reminded him of one of the automata that the archaeologist had made in the time when they were still doing shows together: a wonderful, spluttering, jerking, stumbling, flying dragon that breathed fire when controlled from a mobile phone. She had waited her moment, and, in effect phoned the dragon, and the result was the conflagration. Georg asked the guitarist if he knew whether Maria knew. 'Of course, she does,' he said, 'she always knew,' he said.

The Michaelsons

If my mother or father thought we weren't
working hard enough, or we weren't that
bothered or we didn't appreciate how hard
it all was back in this place they came from
but where we never went, this place called
the 'East End', one of them would say,
'You'll end up like the Michaelsons.'

Who were the Michaelsons? We never met
the Michaelsons. It didn't matter. If we weren't
working hard enough – out it came: 'You'll
end up like the Michaelsons'.

'I've never seen poverty like it,' my mother
said. 'They had bed bugs. There were bed
bugs in the tenements. The Michaelsons
had bed bugs. That's how poor they were.'
So we didn't end up like the Michaelsons.

Yiddish and the Tower of London

My mother said that she wanted to take me
to the Tower of London. She often took me
places. I think it reminded her of how she
thought she had bettered herself. She used
to spend hours in the Bethnal Green Museum.
She told me it was her university. She went
there, she said, so she didn't have to listen
to the *meshpukhe* (relatives) who came over to
play cards in the back room swearing at each
other in Yiddish. My father liked swearing in
Yiddish. They argued about it. My father would
mutter something like '*Chaddich im loch.*' 'Don't
say that!' my mother would say to him. 'What did
he say?' I would say. 'Don't tell him, Harold,'
I had to wait for her to die to find out what it
meant. I don't mean that the day she died
I asked him what '*Chaddich im loch*' meant.
I waited for about 30 years. He told me then.
And I was glad to know.

But maybe she took me to the Tower of London so
that I wouldn't end up swearing in Yiddish.
I loved the Tower of London but one time we
went there was a man with greasy hair, stripped
to the waist who asked people to put him in a sack,
tie him up with chains, stick two swords through
the chains and leave him on the ground to see
if he could escape. He seemed so brave and
dangerous. You could see him riving about inside
the sack. Mum said that we should move on, we
hadn't been inside the White Tower yet but I
pleaded with her to stay to see if he could get
out of the sack. I was sure that he wouldn't be
able to and we would have to unlock the chains
for him. But he went on rolling about on the ground

inside the sack and bit by bit it all got looser and
out he crawled. He was even more greasy now
and he came round with a hat, breathing on us
and I pleaded with Mum again, this time to
give him some money but she wasn't sure she
should but in the end she gave me some and I put
it in his hat. And I was glad because he had been
so brave and dangerous he deserved it.

Muzhik

My mother who had an English
primary school teacher's voice,
and wrote a standard English
she was proud of
loved Shakespeare and Yeats
read me Beatrix Potter and
Winnie the Pooh
in our flat in Pinner,
a place full
of mown parks
men with bowler hats and rolled
umbrellas treading in long lines
to or from the station
on the Metropolitan line,
shops called 'Pat's Pantry'
and the 'Old Oak Tea Rooms',
used to call me 'muzhik'.

It was a gap in the curtain
through which I could see
the mountains and plains
of Russia
winters that froze the bones
and where Napoleon and Hitler's boots
turned to ice.

'Are you alright, muzhik?' she'd say,
never saying a word
about her little boy
who died before me.

I'm Not American

One day
my grandmother
packed her bags
in America
gathered up her children:
got on a boat
and came to England.

There's a photo of
my grandmother
with her three children
on board the boat
that came to England.
They are standing or sitting still.
The boat is moving,
taking them from America to England.

They are standing or sitting still.
Their world is changing:
no more America
London, here they come.
My Dad is one of those three children
standing still for the photo.
He is changing.
In a few days time
he will land in England
and that's where he'll live
from then on.

I'm not American.

Crucify Him

I sat every Easter at school
hearing how the Jews killed Jesus
and just took it that we did bad.

Then Hyam Maccoby pointed out
that the Romans were in charge.
They loved doing that crucifixion thing.
I hadn't noticed.

Customary

I remember my dad
reading George Macbeth's poetry textbook
for 6th formers:
'Eliot's antisemitism was customary for the time.'

'It wasn't "customary" in our house,'
my dad said.

A Little One

My dad was thought
to be stroppier than many.
A colleague of his
described someone
as 'a nasty little Jew'.
My dad interrupted and said,
'Do you know
any other kind of little Jew?'

Food

If you had asked me
in 1956
which of the foods
on my grandmother's table
would become universally loved,
I would have said:
chopped herring.
It turns out
I didn't get that right.

Suburbs

In the beginning
in the suburbs
there was
only macaroni.

Tapioca
Semolina
Raspberry jam
in sago.
How do you start
A pudding race?
All you do is sago.

Where is blancmange?
What happened?
Where did it go?

Pedant

My father was a linguist
and a very non-pedantic linguist.
He wasn't pedantic about anything
apart from cheese cake.
There was only one cheese cake
that was cheese cake.

All the other cheese cakes weren't
cheese cake.

Mother

My mother used to defend me
from my father and brother
if they were taking the mick
or having a go at me.
'Leave him alone, he's tired,'
she'd say.
'Michael hasn't had a wash,'
my brother would say.
'Leave him alone, he's tired,'
my mother would say.

Perhaps
it could go on my grave:
'Leave him alone, he's tired.'

My Mum and the Flower

My dad said that my mum had some secrets.
'One time', he said, 'when she was a girl
at school they said that it was 'Harvest Festival'
and all the children had to bring in flowers.

Well, remember,' said my dad,
'your mother's family were very poor,
they couldn't just go out and buy flowers
and they didn't have a garden
they just had a back yard.
Now all this made your mother ashamed.
She didn't want to be the kid in the class
who didn't bring in flowers.
And she wanted to fit in.
So, do you know what she did?
She slipped into the Park,
 the one just in front of the
Bethnal Green Museum
and she nicked a flower.
Now, don't tell her I've told you that.
She still feels bad about it
but you see she was so worried
about going to school and
being the only one who didn't have
a flower that she was desperate.
So she nicked one from the park.
Now don't tell her I told you about it.
And don't ever tell anyone, will you?'

'No.'

My Dad and his Uncle Sam

When my dad was a boy
he shared a bedroom with
his Uncle Sam.
He didn't talk to his Uncle Sam

'Why not?' I said.
'Because I brought a hat home
from the market
and he turned it inside out and
back again.'
'And you didn't talk to him
because of that?'
'Yes.'
'Ever? You didn't ever talk to him
ever again?'
'That's it.'

'So when you went to bed
how did you decide who would
switch out the light.'
'We didn't have a light.
There was no electricity in the
bedrooms. There were candles.'
'So who decided who would
blow out the candles?'
'We had one each.'

'Just as well.
Otherwise you would have had
to talk to him.'

Census

The census man came round and said
what are you? I said that I don't fill in that
bit because it's always used against people.
He said that's not true, he said he always
filled it in and look at me. I looked at him.
He was black. I said, no I don't fill it in and
he said that he would fill it in for me. I said,
you can't do that because that would be
you defining me. He said that he could do
that, if the occupier would not say what he
was. I said, what will you put me down as?
He said he would put white. I said, well actually
I'm Jewish. He said that comes under religion. I
said I know it's a religion. He said I can put you
down for that under religion, then? I said, well
you can't actually because I'm not a religious
Jew. He said, then you're not Jewish. I said,
I am and he said, I don't have Jewish under
this other part of the form. No, I said, that's
because someone somewhere decided that
I can't call myself Jewish on the form. Well,
he said, I'm afraid that's nothing to do with me.
No, I know it's nothing to do with you, it's do with
people who don't want me to be counted as Jewish.
He said, Mmm. I said, have you got Irish there?
He said, Yes, are you Irish? I said, No, I'm not
Irish but some people who are not Irish say they are
Irish even though they're not born in Ireland,
it's a bit like that with me, only I'm not Irish. Oh, he
said, where were you born, because we could put that.
I said I was born in Harrow, I don't think that's a country.
No, he said, it's not, but I thought if you were
born in Israel I could say you were Israeli. Yes,
I said, but I wasn't born in Israel. No, he said,
you were born in Harrow. That's it, I said, Harrow.

Mr Mensh

I'm not sure that the estate of Roger Hargreaves would give permission but sometimes I lie in bed imagining a special series to go with the *Mr Men* books: Mr Mensh books, a tribute to my parents and all the words they called me.

Mr Shlump	the guy who walks about in clothes he's been wearing all week.
Mr Shloch	the guy who walks about in clothes he's been wearing all year
Mr Mommser	the guy who you don't want to know.
Mr Shpilkes	the guy who's always worried
Mr Tsirres	the guy who's got reason to be worried because he's in trouble
Mr Shtuch	the guy who's also in trouble but it's a bit more trouble
Mr Dr'erd	the guy who's in even more trouble
Mr Mittandring	the guy who's in even more trouble
Mr Dreck	the guy who's crap
Mr Nebbish	the guy who looks like he's turned everything into crap
Mr Varkakhte	the guy who looks like he's crapped himself
Mr Bubkes	the guy who talks rubbish
Mr Pisher	he guy who is rubbish
Mr Bubbele	the guy who is so much of a mummy's boy he's a grandmother's boy
Mr Shmerel	the guy who's a bit of a fool
Mr Shlemiel	the other guy who's a bit of a fool
Mr Shmendrik	and another guy who's a bit of fool
Mr Kvell	the guy who's proud of his son for having made some soup
Mr Kvetsh	the guy who moans about the soup
Mr Chup	the guy who slurps the soup
Mr Shmalts	the guy who's dribbled the soup down his front
Mr Shnorrer	the guy who wants your soup

Mr Chap	the guy who grabs your soup
Mr Chazze	the guy who can't stop having soup
Mr Shmooze	the guy who sweet-talks you to get your soup off you
Mr Zhuzh	the guy who can turn a lousy soup into a good soup
Mr Knakke	the guy who thinks he knows more than your son about how to make soup
Mr Meshugge	the guy who talks nonsense about the soup
Mr Kibbitz	the guy who wants to have a chat while you're having the soup
Mr Yachner	the guy who can't stop talking about the soup
Mr Gantse Magilla	the guy who talks about every single thing that's in the soup
Mr Gubba	the guy who tells you how to make the soup
Mr Ganuf	the guy who nicks your soup
Mr Shtum	the guy who keeps quiet about the guy who nicked your soup
Mr Kishkes	the guy who says that soup gives him a belly-ache
Mr Greps	the guy who has his soup and burps
Mr Fotz	the guy who has his soup and farts
Mr Gantse Macher	the guy who owns the soup factory
Mr Bocher	the guy who's reading books about the soup.

Ridley and Latimer

My father, atheist, Communist, Jewish, liked
to sing 'I'm the man, the very fat man who
waters the workers' beer', a song in Yiddish,
about a Rabbi who got drunk, *Buddy Can
You Spare a Dime, Avanti Popolo*... and
'Last week down our alley came a toff
Nice old geezer with a nasty cough.
Sees my missus, takes his topper off
In a very gentlemanly way!
"Ma'am" says he, "I 'ave some news to tell,
Your rich uncle Tom of Camberwell,
Popp'd off recent, which it ain't a sell,
Leaving you 'is little donkey shay."
"Wot cher!" all the neighbours cried,
"Who yer gonna meet, Bill
Have yer bought the street, Bill?"
Laugh! I thought I should 'ave died.
Knock'd 'em in the Old Kent Road!'

He would also on occasions summon up
the martyring of Bishop Ridley and Bishop
Latimer, both of them burnt at the stake in 1555.
At that very moment, Bishop Latimer
is thought to have said something which
inspired my father to recite, 400 years later
at the breakfast table, on a car journey or
when looking into the embers of the fire on a
camping holiday in Wales:

'Be of good cheer, Master Ridley, and play the
man; we shall this day light such a candle in
England, as I hope, by God's grace, shall never
Be put out.'

Poetry and Noise

One way I got to know that there
was something called poetry came
from my father. Once every so often
there was a programme on the radio
called, 'Poets reading their own poems'.
It came on what was called in those days
the 'Third Programme'. My father – who
we always called 'Harold' – (as a Communist
he thought 'Dad' and 'Daddy' were 'bourgeois')
would see this poetry programme coming up
in the *Radio Times*.

'See this, Con,' he'd say to my Mum (who we
were allowed to call 'Mum'), 'it's poets reading
their own poems, I'm sure the boys would
like that.' Would we? Would we? Really?

So, come Sunday, we would troop off to the
Front Room, sit down in front of the altar of
the radio to listen to 'Poets reading their own
poems'. (You have to imagine this, said in
one of those 1950s, strangulated BBC voices
where the 'o' of 'Poets' sounds more like the
'eur' of 'liqueur'.)

Half way through the programme the presenter
would say, 'And now in this programme of
peu-ets reading their own peu-ems, we have
a very rare recording of the peu-et, WB Yeats
reading his peu-em, "The Lake Isle of Innisfree".
Before we play you this recording, we would
draw your attention to two things: the rather
poor quality, as it was recorded on wax cylinders;
and the rather strange incantatory style of
delivery of the peu-et, WB Yeats,

William Butler Yeats now reading his
peu-em, Lake Isle of Innis... free.' And you
could imagine the presenter pushing out his
bottom lip as he said, 'free'.

Then you would hear, pchrrrr, pchrrrr,
pchrrrr, pchrrrr of the wax cylinder and
following that, the far off, high pitched,
declamatory voice of Yeats calling out
across an imaginary valley, with a voice
located somewhere half way between Belfast
and Oxford: 'I will arise now and go to Innisfreeeeee...'

Our father would be nodding seriously, utterly
gripped by this but my brother and I would
be glancing at each other desperately trying
not to laugh.

In the end we got it up as a take-off.
We practised it in the bedroom. I would cup my
hands and do the wax cylinder noise:
pchrrrr, pchrrrr, pchrrrr
and my brother would rock his head back
and call out to the neighbourhood of Pinner,
'And I will arise now and go to Innisfree...'

But when do you do a take-off like that?

Breakfast.

Harold couldn't stand any noise at breakfast.
In fact, he couldn't stand much noise at all.
But if he wanted to get me and my brother
to be quiet he didn't shout, 'Be quiet!',
he didn't use the Yiddish word, 'Shtum!'
He just put his hand up to the side of his
face and said in a tone of quiet horror,
'The noise!' It looked as if there was

something going on inside his head
it was giving him a great deal of pain
and his hand was trying to reach it.

So picture the moment.
Breakfast.

He would arrive down still wearing his
pyjamas. He didn't wear a dressing-gown.
Bourgeois. He wore his old American Army
great coat lining. It had no buttons, no sleeves
and only just about came down to his knees.
He didn't wear slippers. Also bourgeois –
counter-revolutionary even. He just wore
his shoes. No socks. Just shoes.

Pyjamas, great coat lining and shoes.

It must have been great for my Mum.
Keep the old embers glowing...

Anyway, he arrived in the kitchen door
headed off across the floor. Anything in his
way, he would kick to one side, flopped
himself down and opened up the newspaper.
One moment you had a dad, and the next
thing all you had was the newspaper.
Where did Harold go?
I dunno, he turned into a newspaper.

And that was it. Apart from one thing. His hand.
Every so often, his hand would come out
from behind the paper, head off across
the table to find the coffee cup. The Hand
always knew where the coffee cup was.
My brother and I would sit there staring at The Hand.
Watching it come out, reach the cup and
go back behind the paper. The paper stayed
in exactly the same shape.

One time my brother put his fingers to his lips,
leaned forward and very carefully moved
the coffee cup and sat back.

Out came The Hand, but when it couldn't find
the cup, it flapped about, there were indignant
noises from behind the paper and next thing
he peeped out, grunted about things not being
where they should be and he went back to the paper.

Then my brother pointed at me, and silently showed
me how I should cup my hands... and that he
was going to do the Lake Isle of Innisfree.
I shook my head. Too dangerous.
No, no, he nodded.
So, I cupped my hands, 'Pchrrrr, pchrrrr,
pchrrrrr!' and my brother threw his head back,
'I will arise now and go to Innisfreeeeee'
Down came the newspaper, up went my
father's hand to his face, 'The noise!!!'
and my brother was in there with,
'But it's poetry, Harold. Poetry.'

Reading for Pleasure

Reading for Pleasure for all cannot be achieved by one agency alone: not schools alone, not libraries alone, not voluntary organisations alone. It has to be a many-headed Policy from all these. Every voluntary initiative about reading for Pleasure is welcome. But it's not enough to reach all. It needs to be a cultural in-school and out-of-school Policy.

I
Haven't
Ever
Said
That
One
Thing
Only
Solves
The
Problem
Of
How
We
Can
Enable
Reading
For
Pleasure
For
All.
And
I
Don't
Blame
Parents.

It
Gets
Us
Nowhere.

Btw I've sat face to face on different occasions with four Education ministers: Balls, Knights, Coaker, Gibb plus Culture Minister Hodge trying to convince them that Reading for Pleasure needs to be 'Policy' and I've totally failed to convince them.

The problem is that 'reading books for Pleasure in your spare time' was never made part of 'education' so no one makes it 'policy'. But every research on it shows that education is enabled by RfP in spare time! It needs to be policy so ALL can benefit.

I notice on the comments thread after my article about reading for pleasure in the Guardian how soon it attracts the 'blame parents' lobby. Do they think the state shouldn't do education? The RfP argument is that RfP should be part of education. Not a voluntary annexe to it.

It.
Can't.
All.
Be.
Done.
With.
Voluntary.
Projects.

It's not a matter of implementing one thing. It's about a cultural policy.

Teacher librarians, librarians, children's librarians, school librarians, the school library service, the YLG, the SLA, librarians, librarians, librarians. This should be the backbone of in-school and out-of-school education.

What we read and how we read as children is not trivial or 'childish'. It's these books that contribute to our patterns of thinking, dreaming, hoping, fearing, yearning for... and of course our patterns of reading and understanding the printed word for the rest of our lives.

Meaning is also conveyed through 'prosody' – the rhythms, sound-patterns, repetitions, variations in the musicality of a text. Dickens uses this a lot when distinguishing between the discursive ironic narration and the poetic descriptive one.

Parents who share hundreds of picture books with their under-5s enable their children to make cognitive leaps through trying to interpret the logic and meanings suggested by the unstated differences between the pictures and the text.

Reading for Pleasure works because books work. Books work because they invite interpretation = the play of speculation, reflection, prediction, affirmation, surprise, deduction, analysis, wonder, empathy, fear, hope, horror, sensuality, conceptual thinking, memory... and more.

The big irony of recent educational change is that parents who, at home, can use 'progressive' non-cramming educational methods of: cooperation, invention, discussion, children doing planning, investigation, discovery, and interpretation bestow huge advantages on their children!

It's not simply a matter of 'teaching children to read and write'. There is the question of who owns literacy. Who leaves school thinking that they own literacy, that writing is something that they own and control and use in many different ways according to their needs? How can we help children own literacy? Publishing and performing, whole school texts, suspending the curriculum, open interpretation using open questions like 'what were you most affected by in this book? Is there anything in the book where that reminded you of something in your life? How? Why? Is there anything in the book that reminded you of something you've ever read or heard or seen on TV or in the cinema? How? Why? Have you got any questions you'd like to ask someone in the book? Have you got any questions for the author? Can you answer any of those questions?... and reading for pleasure...

The best help you can give for writing (schools or wherever): imitation, invention, investigation, interpretation and audience. Ie saying 'we can write like that, make stuff up, wonder why, discuss and share.'

The danger [irony alert!] of silent reading is that it doesn't provide instant data, it provokes thought and interpretation and when it provokes talk, this quickly leads to higher order thinking, independent of direct instruction.

It needs to be 'policy' because we want it to be 'reading for pleasure FOR ALL.' Like health used to be done by charities but it meant not everyone got it. Reading for pleasure should simply be part of education ie what we all do.

When I say 'education' – I don't only mean 'schools' – I mean in-school and – just as importantly out-of-school. This needs to bring together the kind of thinking that goes on inside the voluntary bodies with those in education.

The comments thread following my article in an article I wrote for the *Guardian* about 'Reading for Pleasure' is full of parent-blaming stuff, which in effect says, 'Well, there's nothing you can do and there's no point in doing it.' Why do people do that?

Reading works to enable us to think because when we read we make comparisons between life and the book, between the book and other books, and between things in the book. These acts of comparison are at the least a first step towards making generalised and/or abstract thoughts.

Reading for Pleasure works because books work. Books work because they invite interpretation = the play of speculation, reflection, prediction, affirmation, surprise, deduction, analysis, wonder, empathy, fear, hope, horror, sensuality, conceptual thinking, memory... and more.

Reading for Pleasure is 360 degrees. Every part of in-school and out-of-school policy has to contribute and co-operate.

The interesting thing about fiction, drama and poetry is that more often than not, they involve some kind of marriage between ideas and feelings attached to beings ('characters) that we come to care about.

Reading is one of the easiest ways in which we get hold of the strategies and procedures of continuous prose (CP). CP is very different from speech, dialogue and inner speech. CP carries the language of law, administration, humanities and science.

When we read, we relate our interpretation of the text with our experience of life and experience of the texts we know. This 'comparison-making' is the central component of 'interpretation'. We do this with dialogue, but with reading it is slower and more prolonged.

Browsing and choosing are essential parts of reading for pleasure. We learn how to scan and make judgements on what we have scanned. We learn if we can indeed judge a book by its cover and if not, why not. We find out ways to books we want and need.

Dick Leith

1947–2011

The string between us got longer
and longer
but I promise you
I carried your wheezy laugh
with me in all that time,
along with your face near the moment of
our Finals exam
when you told me how
the night before,
you had dreamed
you stood on the roof of the library building
and the examiners
(who would soon be poring
over our translations
of Old and Middle English)
threw you off.

Reading is a meeting of dramas

The other day I heard myself say to a teachers' meeting that rather than worry about a child's 'level' or supposed 'lack' of knowledge, think of how a book or poem might relate to that child's psychodrama. Pompous I know. But I kinda believe that.

What I meant is that every one of us, no matter our background, no matter what 'level' we have been put on, lives a life that is in its own way a drama. Books and poems and plays are dramas. When we read or view the two dramas (our own and the one in the book or poem or drama) intermingle. We relate them. This applies whether we have read 100s of books and have education pouring out of our ears, or if we are 6 years old and been designated special needs or whatever. We all have that drama of how we relate to the world and to other people. This is what we bring to books, plays and poems.

As authors or teachers it's our job, then, to think of the psychodramas – in the child/children and in the books, plays and poems and figure out how these intermingle and inter-relate.

That's what I meant when I heard myself say that.

Found Poem: a Reading Wall-chart for Children from the 1840s

A man met a mad ram.
Do not let a fat cat sit on a bed.
Do not let it do so.
A fat cat ran at a rat and fed on it.
A red rod is for me, and a fat cat is for me.
A fan is for a man.
A lad ran for a bat for me.
A red rod is for a bad lad, and for me if I am bad.
A red rod and a fat cat.

School Visit

Me in school: 'Down behind the dustbin,
I met a dog called Felicity.
It's a bit dark, down here,
they cut off my –'

Child: 'Tail!'

Writing

The key thing to remember
is that no document about writing
produced by government
has ever been written by anyone
who writes anything
other than documents
like documents on how to write.

Tick-box Marking

Tick box marking says 'personification'.
If you write an alternative expression
like 'animating'
or 'anthropomorphism' – no mark.
If you forget to say:
'and the effect on the reader is' – no mark.
(Who is this 'reader' who keeps
experiencing effects?)

My advice is:
fudge English exams.
Think of this 'reader' as a superhero
who always gets the effect.
Exams are about guessing
what superhero reader thinks.

Book Festivals

The thing about book festivals,
children come and hear authors
and ask authors questions
and there are no tests or exams.
The children just get to think
and reflect and wonder and ponder –
on their own or with friends or family.
How come this sort of thing is allowed?

Grammar

Given that the 'grammar' system
they have invented is
abstract, complex
and doesn't refer to context
or social function;
given that it
keeps changing the terminology;
given that the grammarians disagree,
someone somewhere will always be 'wrong'.

Ideal therefore for pointless exams.

Envy

Rows of silent Chinese children
seated at desks,
heads bowed over high-stakes tests
that will determine their future.

When it comes to China,
Tories have serious tyranny-envy.

Answers

There'll never be a SATs question
on why Humpty fell off the wall.
Too many possible answers.

Writing

The easiest way to write
is to find a piece of writing
and change it
so that it says things
that you would like to read.

Same Difference

Skills – knowledge?
Knowledge – skills?

I dissected a body
when I did medicine:
we got anatomical knowledge
by dissecting.
We learnt how to dissect
using anatomical knowledge.

Damian Hinds

*'When you leave school, hard and stressful things come along.
Learning about what can be stressful episodes is part of the
preparation for later life.'*

Is there a principle here?
Whatever horrible experience
we might have in later life
should be put on the school curriculum
or be part of how the curriculum is taught.

For many people, the tedium of work
is one feature of adult life.
Rather than leaving it to chance,
or just occasional moment of tedium
can we make it policy that school
should be tedious
all the time?

One of the results of government policy
since the financial crisis of 2008
is that more and more people are finding it
hard to make ends meet.
Teachers tell me that
more and more children are arriving at school hungry.

I gather there are teachers
giving children breakfasts
to ensure they get enough calories a day.
Surely this is a mistake?
There is every chance
that such children will end up in jobs
that don't pay enough
(or they have no jobs)
and they won't have enough to eat.
It would be much better
to keep the children hungry
to prepare them for later life.

Bad Grammar

Is an invented description.

If a phenomenon in language
(something said or written)
doesn't fit the description,
which is wrong?
The phenomenon
or the description?

Hear

One of the ways we find out
what we don't know
is hearing
what other people say
they don't know.

More Grammar

The grammar
that has to be taught
in primary schools
doesn't teach
beyond the sentence
into a whole piece of writing
nor out into the world.

It's imprisoned
between a capital letter
and the next full stop,
with functions it talks about
created
as an abstract representation
of processes
that have no reference point
other than to themselves.

A Child

A child
a book
a read
a chat.
This is the way the mind grows.
Not with a test
but a tale.

How do Books Help us Think?

They invite us
to relate what we read
to what we know.
We make comparisons and analogies
without being asked to.
We do it
in order to follow the meaning.

These are steps towards
abstract thought:
generalisations, categories.

Books are enablers.

The Arts

The Arts are a waste of time:
all they tell us are things like
how to understand yourself,
your place in the world,
how materials work,
how society works,
how to co-operate to get things done,
resilience,
optimism,
powers of reflection,
interpretation,
holding your nerve...

Read

Every time you read,
you learn something.
It may be obvious.
It may be mysterious.
It may be seeing something new.
It may be that you're reminded
of something in your mind.
It may be the possible.
It may be the impossible.
Does that sound good?

I think it does.

The Data have Landed

First they said they needed data
about the children
to find out what they're learning.
Then they said they needed data
about the children
to make sure they are learning.
Then the children only learnt
what could be turned into data.
Then the children became data.

Standards

[Smile at everyone]
Thank you very much for giving me the opportunity today
to talk to you about standards.
[pause for effect]
You will have seen in the press a good deal of alarmist headlines
about so-called cuts in funding and provision. Let me leave to one
side the matter of whether these really are or are not cuts.
[look up at everyone to make sure that this point is understood]
The issue for all teachers, parents and children is standards. So
whether there is or is not less money in the pot, what counts is the
standard of education that our children are getting.
[if necessary repeat this point with a gesture with the right hand]
And let me make it quite clear right from the start that when I say
standards I don't mean the standard of education. What I mean is
the standards reached by children in the tests and exams they do
right from the off and all the way through their school lives. It
would be a great mistake to confuse the matter.
[prepare for a change of tone, be sneery but not too sneery]
Yes, of course, due to the last Labour government's complete
mismanagement of the economy, we've all had to tighten our belts
and in the case of schools, it might have been that we've even lost
the belts themselves, so there isn't much left to tighten.
[pause for laughter].
As a result, I'm told that there are schools cutting back on school
journeys, art, music, teaching assistants – even the school day itself.
[appear slightly regretful at this point]
But this has nothing to do with standards.
[right hand forceful movement]
I repeat, standards are the standards achieved in the tests and
exams. So long as they stay stable or better, there is no decline in
standards.

Now some might say that the tests and exams are regularised and moderated so that we have comparable outcomes. I apologise if that sounds like jargon, that may not mean a great deal to everyone listening to this.
[sincere]
In effect, it means that once the exam results are in, a group of highly trained
[try to sound like Michael Gove at his best here]
mathematicians look at the results overall and if there is any sense that there is slippage, they make sure that the results come out with the overall scores we want.
[purposeful]
This way we know that standards are maintained.

So, what I say to all the prophets of doom out there is: never mind the standard, focus on the standards.
[raise the voice at the end of the sentence and pause for applause]
Yes, never mind the standard, focus on the standards.
[stay standing while people applaud.]

How to End Austerity

1. Stand up and say 'Austerity is over'.
2. Go into radio and TV studios and say, 'Austerity is over'.
3. Rely on people in radio and TV studios
   and in newspapers to say,
   'Austerity is over'.
4. That's it.
5. But is austerity over?
6. No. Goodnight.

Statement

'As Minister for Telling Everyone That Things Are OK Really, I'd like to repeat that inequality is not really a problem. Apart from anything else, it's clear that income inequality is coming down. This means that we don't take into consideration such things as tax avoidance, wealth acquired through rent, sale of assets and dividends from shares which has enabled people to become extraordinarily wealthy. But then we don't want people to focus on that sort of thing because it breeds envy. In the meantime I'm going to keep going on about how inequality is coming down, and life is getting better for all. Thank you.'

Low Wages

Capitalism discovers that low wages don't buy the stuff that capitalism sells. So capitalism lends money to people so that people can buy stuff that capitalism sells. Capitalism discovers that high debt is fine so long as people can afford to pay the interest on the debt. Capitalism finds that things might get tricky if people can't afford to pay the interest...

Social Mobility

I love the ladder of social mobility:
up we go
working hard to better ourselves,
or staying where we are
because we are not good enough.
Presumably,
there are some people up the top
not working hard
who will slip down to make way
for those going up...
Though they seem to forget to mention
that there's a lift alongside the ladder,
carrying a special group
who zoom to the top floor
whenever they want,
carrying their inherited wealth,
tax havens and private education.
You can hear them shouting
across to the people on the ladder
'Work harder, pass your exams!'

Zoom zoom they go in their lift.
Zoom zoom.

I'm Not on the List, I'm Not on the List

I'm not on the list
I'm not on the list
All I have to do is tell them
if I know someone who should be on the list.

If I don't tell them
that I know someone who should be on the list,
then I'll be on a list of people
who don't help them make the list.

And people in my family
will be on a list of people
in families of people
who don't help them make the list
of people who should be on the list.

And people (who people in my family know)
will be on a list of people
who know people in the family of someone
who didn't help them make the list of people
who should be on the list.

So, if you're not on the list
or the list of the people
who don't help them make the list
or the list of people who know people who
don't help them make the list
you're OK.
It's all OK
It's going to be all right.

It Wasn't Immigrants

For Labour MPs going in hunt of votes by raising fears about 'non-British workers'.

It wasn't immigrants who crashed the banks.
It wasn't immigrants who said we had to tighten our belts.
It wasn't immigrants who cut a million jobs from the public sector.
It wasn't immigrants who slapped on the wage cap.
It wasn't immigrants who stoked up the housing market.
It wasn't immigrants who stopped building council houses.
It wasn't immigrants who cut the budgets for schools and the NHS.
It wasn't immigrants who closed down Fords Dagenham.
It wasn't immigrants who hide billions in tax havens.
It wasn't immigrants who spend billions on bombs.

Pointing the finger at immigrants is several times wrong: it's scapegoating the ills of capitalism on to people who are victims.

We'll never build a better society by singling out people on the basis that they've moved country, are born somewhere else, or speak languages other than the ones of the state they find themselves in.

Capitalism runs the whole system, and this produces people who suffer one way or another.

We build a better society by linking up those who suffer and those who sympathise with those who suffer.

Meanwhile the system can move its wealth wherever it wants by pressing keys on a keyboard.

Those who suffer and those who sympathise with them must have the right to defend themselves and one way is to move.

The moment we hoist barriers to moving, we hand more power to those who are running the system which causes the suffering, and we create elites and persecutions amongst ourselves.

There is no hope for us to build a better society on that basis.

What the poem also suggests that part of scapegoating is a system to invite us to blame the wrong cause.

I've listed reasons and ways in which people's lives have been substantially harder as a result of explicit government policy and/or the actions of extremely wealthy people.

These causes for people's suffering are nothing to do with the movement of people.

The sum of the factors in my poem far, far, far outweigh any apparent or so-called disadvantage accruing from the movement of people – and let's not forget the millions of Brits who move at the same time, to places where they become migrants.

'Mass' migration works in all directions, with people with different needs, skills and abilities trying to find places where they can make a living under a global system that they don't own or control.

Even the phrase 'putting pressure on public services' trotted out by Tories and Labour is obscene in its deceit.

The greatest pressure on public services comes from decades of underfunding and cuts and privatisations done so that – in theory – capitalists could have a bigger freer market. For what? Who's benefited from that?

The great struggle that capitalists are involved in is competition with each other.

They will take any steps necessary to win those competitions, all the way to war.

Our job is to unite those who are exploited, those who suffer, those who are oppressed, those seeking to defend themselves in order to lessen the burden in the short term and to built a better society in the long term.

Any scapegoating will make that job harder, or worse: it builds a lop sided society in which some are more equal than others, just as George Orwell said.

Not There

In schools, children tell me of visiting
their uncles, aunts and cousins or brothers
or sisters of grandmas and grandads in
Jamaica, Bangladesh, Cyprus... They tell me
how their relatives spoke and what the
mangos were like. They talk of street
festivals: a man dressed up and people
sang 'De devil day tap-tap, De devil day
tap-tap'... fishing, and climbing trees.
They tell me about words and accents,
mosquitoes and snakes. I think how I
would like to tell them about me doing the
same. How I'd been to France or Poland
visiting great-aunts and uncles, listened to
them speaking French, Yiddish and German,
ate chopped liver and warm *cholla*. But there's
no one to see. In my lifetime, there
never has been. I read of cities where the
meshpukhe (relatives) mended clocks,
sold nuts and bolts. I look at a picture of
two aunts walking arm in arm with a young
man wearing a cap – he's the son of one of
them. They're in a street, laughing, with high
blocks of flats behind them. The name of the
city has changed. In Paris and Sedan two
names are carved on to monuments. In both
cities: 'Rosen'. I'll tell the children that.

Kashoggi

In an official statement released today, the Saudi regime have revealed that deaths in Yemen are caused by civilians leaping into the air and colliding with Saudi defence systems.

It's emerging that Kashoggi died from a condition known as 'Interrogation'. With this condition, no matter what is done to them, by whom or how, it's the patient's fault if they die.

And it's now emerging that so-called 'beheadings' in Saudi Arabia are caused by outbreaks of people running very fast towards an axe. The British Government sends condolences to the Saudi regime.

The latest news is that when Kashoggi walked into the embassy he was already dead.

Nation

The Nation State Law of Israel states that
it is the place where Jews 'self-determine'.
It does not mention the 25% of the people
of Israel who are not Jews.

The nation is made up of its people. The
Nation State Law is the Law for the people.
But not all the people are mentioned.
They are un-mentioned. They are the people
who are not seen by the Law. They do not
exist. In fact, they so do not exist
that it is not even mentioned that they do not
exist. They are nothing. In fact, it is not even
mentioned that they are a nothing. In fact,
I haven't even said this. This is not a
statement. There is nothing here. You
have not read it. You will not mention the
unmentioned people when talking about the
Law.

Because the Law does not mention the people
who are not mentioned, the Law cannot harm
the people not mentioned. It does not
discriminate against them because they are
not mentioned in the Law.

You may mention how this Law is a Law that
does not discriminate against any people but
you may not mention any people who are not
mentioned.

Analysis

Media analysis of the Russian Revolution is hardly getting beyond the idea that
a)   it happened
b)   some bad stuff happened later
c)   QED the RR was bad.
d)   PS Lenin had bad breath. And shaved his beard off.

I think we should apply this method to some other areas of history. How about Luther and the Reformation?
a)   it happened
b)   some bad stuff happened later (wars, famine, persecution, tyrannical regimes)
c)   QED it was bad.
d)   sorted.
e)   PS Luther talked a lot about farting.

Dear British People

I know that this message will come to you as a surprise. I am the person in charge of the country of the United Kingdom. I hope that you will not expose or betray this trust and I am confident that I am about to repose on you for our mutual benefit.

I need your urgent assistance in transferring a sum of money from you, who are the nearest persons to our deceased welfare state who died in a banking crash in 2008, into the account of some extremely rich people within 10 or 14 banking days.

I don't want the money to go into government treasury as an abandoned fund. Please I would like you to keep this proposal as a top secret.

I am expecting your urgent response as soon as you receive my message

Best Regards,

Theresa May

Disabled

At some point
we are all disabled.
Maybe from birth.
Maybe a bit later.
Maybe for years,
maybe for months.
Maybe for weeks.
Maybe for days.
Maybe for hours.
Maybe for minutes.
Maybe for seconds.
All of us.
It's us.
All of us.
Disability is us.

A&E

As part of a new efficiency drive
the government is giving hospital A&E
a much-needed shake-up. After years
of overcrowding, the government have
what may well be a solution to the crisis:
an appointment system for Accident and
Emergency Departments. This is how it
will work: if you think you are likely to
be knocked down in the road, fall out of a
second storey window, walk into a sharp
object, or swallow some bleach, then simply
call your local hospital A&E department,
tell them which accident or emergency you
think you are likely to experience and they
will find you a slot for you in that day's schedule.
No more confusion or panic, no more
red lights flashing, and alarms going off.
Instead, when you have your accident,
simply make arrangements to get yourself
to the hospital and a team of world-class
medics will be on hand.

Ed Balls on *This Week*

Just been watching *This Week*. Ed Balls has become an endangered species – not because he's been hunted down but because the climate's changed. He sits in the corner like a rhino that can't stand up and issues long plaintive mutters that no one understands or even tries to understand. There must be a comfortable but useless stable for him somewhere: like becoming the chair of a small charity that deals with people who wish they were cats.

Worried

Most mornings
I wake up worried about
how David Cameron is.
We don't seem to hear from him.
I fear that he may
have fallen on hard times.
I just hope he's alright
and is not too proud to talk.

Mr Fair

'Fairness is what I've been fighting for all my working life. Watch my new video setting out how I will campaign for a fairer Britain.'
Dominic Raab

One day Mr Fair went for a walk. 'I'm very fair,' he said.

Some poor people looked at the things that Mr Fair had done. He had helped poor people get poorer.

'That's not very fair,' the poor people said.

'Oh yes it is very fair,' said Mr Fair.

Good old Mr Fair.

David Cammeron's Stories

Mr Chump

Auntie Theresa is going to have tea with Mr Chump. I might be aloud to go but Mummie says I must not ask Mr Chump why he is orange. Mr Chump is grate at telling storeys and nun of them are true. It will be fun.

The End

The Trowsers

Borris came over and sed, 'I cant find my trowsers, trowseros non habeo wot wot.' I sed, 'You are wearing them Borris.' I laughed at his funny joke. He went home. Later he sent someone rownd to punch me.

The End

Jerremy

For a bit, I went to a house and had to talk to horrid Jerremy. Once I told him to where proper clothes. Ha ha. Once I told him to just go. Ha ha. In the end I was the one to go and I herd Jerremy say ha ha.

The End

Mr Horrid

Auntie Theresa's going away soon and she says we mustnt let horrid Jerremy in. Auntie says, 'Remember. Everyone hates Mark Cyst. If Jerremy comes to the door, shout, 'Your Mark Cyst!' I sed, 'Is he Mark Cyst?' Auntie sed, 'No, but if everyone thinks he is, he wont get in.'

The End

Auntie

I use to think Auntie Theresa was no good. Now she's gone away, she's startid being nice and coming up with nice ideas. She has startid saying that young peeple are nice and we should be nice to them. So now we all think Auntie Theresa is nice.

The End

Mr Nigel

Nigel Garage has startid popping up on TV again. He speeks very very very loudly and is freinds with some peeple in Europ. He says he doesn't like Europ but he sure likes the Europ peeple who do that arm-in-the-air salutey thing.

The End

The Tummie Upset

One tyme wen I was a littl boy, I had a tummie upset and I was sick all over the floor. 'Now what are we going to do?' mummie said. 'I know,' I said, 'I'll go out of the room and it'll go away.'

The End.

Tony Blair

Please give him at least a tiny bit of media exposure.

Is there a chance, a faint possibility, a smidgeon of an opening, a reasonable opportunity, please, please, please for Tony Blair to have a chat show or platform all of his own, a solo spot, a talk show, a late night spot, a morning talk, a regular interview, a brief appearance, a timely intervention, on any major media outlet or all major outlets, so that we can hear from him regularly, at least once a month, but ideally, more often, once a week, or once a day, or several times a day across several channels, or multiple news slots, a variety of media platforms so that we can for once, just once, hear what his views, thoughts, timely musings are on politics, war, the Middle East, the Labour Party, elections, Jeremy Corbyn, anti-semitism, morality, hope, the will to live, personal wealth, human rights, bigots, socialism, values, community, money, weather, shirts, toilet cleaner, printing ink, acne, the stone age, driving tests, fortune cookies, Jeremy Corbyn, water melons, Jeremy Corbyn, morality, Jeremy Corbyn, personal wealth, Jeremy Corbyn, war, Jeremy Corbyn, Jeremy Corbyn, Jeremy Corbyn and Jeremy Corbyn?

Production Company

'We are a production company providing a variety of top quality, topical news programmes for radio, TV, podcasts and other online platforms and we are looking for any politicians who have been disgraced, caught committing offences of any kind – false expenses claims, libel, lying, deceiving, etc or any politicians who escaped prosecution by making unfounded accusations under parliamentary privilege, any politicians who have lucrative (albeit legal) arrangements with companies who lobby parliament for special treatment of some kind, any politicians who have special relationships with foreign powers, known but not usually declared, any politicians with millions of pounds in tax havens or highly tax-efficient arrangements or if you are a politician who falls into one or other of these categories or anything that sounds similar, we need you urgently to appear in some of our programmes disguised as moderate, sensible, middle-of-the-road, reputable, reasonable, reliable, honest, not particularly wealthy people. We guarantee to make you feel welcome and you will be free to make your points uninterrupted and without any reminder of any of your past or present attachments, associations, misdemeanours, transgressions or crimes. In the event of our being in touch with you, could you please rehearse some accusations of your own, directed at any of the following: Jeremy Corbyn, the Labour Party, Momentum, the Labour Party Front Bench, Diane Abbott, Jeremy Corbyn and Jeremy Corbyn?

Look forward to hearing from you.'

Some Ideas for TV Programmes

6-part: Alastair Campbell and Portillo Walk Disused Railway Lines.

3-hour special: Peace in Our Time. Tony Blair looks at great peace treaties of the past.

Ongoing: Football's a Game of Two Halves: Alistair Campbell picks his fave 45 minutes from the past.

The Principles and the Pauper: Margaret Hodge goes in search of people who've stuck to their principles even if it meant they became poverty-stricken.

Great Constituencies: Chuka Umunna talks to MPs about the country's best constituency to represent.

Moderately Extreme: Alastair Campbell hosts a discussion between two moderates who've taken extreme action in order to be moderate.

Great Tax-Havens of the World: Jacob Rees-Mogg tours the tax havens and finds out how they keep the world going.

Oy Vey: Ian Austin teaches non-Jews like him how to be Jewish.

Right to Remember: present-day leaders take us back to a key moment in their country's history, starting with Marine Le Pen taking us back to the glories of the Vichy years in France.

.

The Unheard: Jeremy Clarkson, Piers Morgan, Rod Little and Richard Littlejohn chat to each other every lunch time about why ordinary guys like them can never get a word in edgeways these days.

The Newcomer: a three-month long series in which Lord Sugar tests anxious, aspiring, people with self-deluded ideas about how they are going to become millionaires, as they compete against each other whilst pretending to be working together. Lord Sugar humiliates them each week.

Changing Places: a popular reality TV show in which Old Etonians go back to Eton and swap houses, finding out what it would have been like if they had been in a different house from the one that they were in when they were at Eton.

Old Tricks, Eugenics: Toby Young and Dominic Cummings show how the planet could be saved in just a few generations with the right breeding practices put in place as soon as possible.

I Bike It: Michael Portillo returns with great bike rides he would do if he rode a bike.

Grandad: a series of profiles of the grandchildren of prominent Nazis talking about the funny foibles, jokes, and quirks of their famous grandfathers.

Scrutony: the great philosopher Roger Scruton casts a critical eye over everything in England that isn't English enough.

Jacob Rees-Hob: in the kitchen with Jacob as he directs his servants to cook him his favourite meals.

The Meaning of Life: 12-part series with Prince Charles in which he tells us what it's all for, ranging over art, music, the origin of the species, the universe, and beyond.

Straw Man: a retrospective look with Jack Straw looking at why he's so dull.

The Day Job: we follow Peter Mandelson as he puts into practice his avowed intent to bring down Jeremy Corbyn every day of his life.

Get Up and Go: David Cameron tells the stories of the some of the great exits of the past, people who just dropped everything and left.

Double Deutsche: Sajid Javid takes us back to that memorable moment at the Deutsche Bank when the Bank was involved in major fiddles.

They Weren't All Bad: Steve Bannon takes us on a trip round the world's great dictators and mass murderers and finds some good things they did.

The Man on the Omnibus: great bus rides with Michael Portillo.

Great Ways to Spend 45 minutes with Alastair Campbell.

Plane Speaking: Michael Portillo goes on some of the great long haul flights of the world, testing his endurance for 8,10, 12 and 14 hour flights, watching movies and levering peanut crumbs out of his crotch.

The Truth and Nothing but the Truth: two news presenters sit at a shiny table getting the latest news from each other, asking each other to talk about the news that they've just talked about.

De-clutter: each week a presenter comes on and explains how the political scene would be better if there was no Labour Party. Guests suggest different ways it can be done.

Rear Window: in depth examination of the life and work of a media magnate in which Michael Gove goes on a journey up the rear end of Rupert Murdoch.

Comma, Comma Chameleon: back to the classroom with Jacob Rees-Mogg where he commands his servants to punctuate properly.

Mock the Weak: each episode, Boris Johnson picks on another minority and comes up with fun ways to humiliate them.

Hard Labour: each week, an expert (who is not in the Labour Party and has never voted Labour and would never vote Labour and doesn't know anyone who votes Labour) tells us what the Labour Party should do.

For Steve's a Jolly Good Fellow: in which journalists queue up to ask Steve Bannon why he's so clever.

Inside Out: a daily series in which Labour Party politicians explain why they shouldn't be in the Labour Party. A year later they come back and explain why they still shouldn't be in the Labour Party.

Full Marx: a fun panel game in which the contestants have to give a talk using the words Marx, Marxist or Marxism as often as possible without ever giving away what the words mean.

Poor Choices: Dominic Raab, Iain Duncan Smith and assorted millionaires go and find some poor people and offer them advice on how to make lifestyle choices to improve their lives.

Kiss me Kate: a fun game in which guests guess who Katie Hopkins hates today. If they get it right, they get to kiss Katie. It's a kind of hate love-in. Fun for all the family.

Lucky Dip with the DUP: Arlene Foster, Nigel Dodds, Sammy Wilson come into the studio to take it in turns to try the Tory Lucky Dip. Winner takes all.

No One Round Here: journalists walk quickly through shopping centres and markets shouting out, 'Anyone here vote for Corbyn?' The camera catches blank faces, people turning away, shaking their heads. Journalist stops, turns, shrugs and says, 'No one supporting Mr Corbyn here.'

Redeeming Feature: journalists discuss whether tyrants and bigots have plus points: e.g. Hitler's moustache, was it well-groomed? Did Stalin have twinkly eyes? Are Trump's suits well-made? Does Boris Johnson eat a good breakfast?

Testing Times: contestants in this lively panel game have to think up new exams for children to do. First week: Nick Gibb, Phonics for Free-year olds.

Join the Club: oligarchs, money-launderers, tax-avoiders , asset-strippers, environment-wreckers and currency speculators come together to discuss what football clubs they would take over if they could and how they can keep their business affairs out of the media.

Fault Towers: rich presenters and rich guests invite poor people into the studio and blame them for being poor.

For Bookmarks Bookshop

following the attack on the shop by a far right group

It looks like we've got
yet another case
of guys out rooting
for the master race
invading a shop,
being a bit of a pain
trying to make 'Britain
Great Again'
by pulling books off shelves,
refusing to leave:
'what a tangled web'
these klutzes weave:
like bumbling old Boris,
what a decent bloke,
just happens to make
a passing joke
while kindly Steve Bannon
speaks for rationalism,
has a platform on *Newsnight*
for his Economic Nationalism.
Nothing to worry about
we just have to keep calm
It's 'Judeo-Christian war
'gainst militant Islam.'
If you think that's just
a load of old testicles,
Netanyahu said that
to the Evangelicals.

So what looks like
just a few books on the floor
is part of a picture that's
telling us much more.
Anytime we think
they're just having a laugh
let's remember the joker
with the toothbrush moustache.
Many thought then
he was just a bit of a pain
who said he'd make
his country great again,
who many thought then
he was just a funny face
not a man who'd convince
you were the master race.

We've been here before
with Griffin and Tyndall
who did their very best
to light and kindle
the fire of fascism
in every street
but last time they tried
they faced defeat.

Come summer, come winter
wind, frost or rain,
we stopped them before
we'll stop them again.

The War of Corbyn's Coat

If Corbyn's coat is wrong,
the others' coats must be right.
The dead cannot see coats.
Day cannot see night.

Hurrah for the warriors of the press!
We know what rocks their boat:
at the sight of a million dead,
they quibble over Corbyn's coat.

Let us praise famous coats,
worn to mourn the dead of war;
worn by those who lead us
as their bombs slay even more.

It's not his coat they hate.
That's not really their cause
What gets up all their noses?
He opposes all their wars.

Let us imagine the day –
or it could perhaps be night.
The politicians start a war
and no one turns up to fight.

Maths

1 wrong Corbyn coat = bad man.
Therefore 1 good coat = good man.
Trump wears a good coat.
Therefore Trump = good man.

Tomorrow's lesson:
SS officers' lovely leathers.

Fossils

My brother works at the Natural
History Museum in London. He's a
fossil. No – sorry, I got that wrong.
He looks after the fossils.
Looks after the fossils? What sort
of job is that? I mean it can't be very
hard, can it? They're just stones.
They don't jump at you, like if you
were looking after a tiger. Imagine
that, you come down in the morning,
there's a tiger. You go up to it, and you
say, 'What do you want to eat?' And the
tiger says, 'YOU!' That would be hard.
No, my brother looks after fossils. I went
into his room forty years ago and there
were four fossils sitting on a shelf. I said,
'What are you doing Brian?' He said,
'Looking after the fossils.' I said, 'They're not
going to jump off the shelf, are they?'
He said, 'You never know. That's what
I'm here for.' I went to his office the other
day and the four fossils were still there.
On the shelf. I said, 'Brian, the fossils
are still there!' And he said, 'Yes.
That's because I was here.'
If ever you find a fossil and
you don't know what it's called,
you might pick it up and
shout at it: 'Dave!' 'Melanie!'
and it doesn't answer – then
you can take it to the Natural
History Museum in London and
you go up to one of the people in uniform
and tell them you've got a fossil
and you don't know its name:

'Dave!', 'Melanie!' – see it doesn't
answer, and they send for my brother,
Doctor Brian Rosen. He lives in a cave
underneath the museum, he wears
a leopard skin bikini and he's got a
great big club, and he comes up
from down below the museum, you'll
hear him coming, 'Ooof!!! Oooof!!!'
and suddenly the big double doors open
in front of you and there he is in his
leopard skin bikini and you can go up
to him and say, 'Hello. I've found a fossil,
and I don't know its name: Dave!
Melanie! See it doesn't answer,' and my
brother takes a magnifying glass out of
his leopard skin bikini bottom and it's
one of those little ones, and he puts it
in his eye and it makes his eye go really
big and he studies it very hard and then
he says, 'No, that's not Dave. It's not
Melanie, that is an ammonite.' Or maybe
he'll say, 'That is a belemnite.' and you'll
be very pleased. And if it's a really, really
good one, do you know what he does
then? He nicks it off you. Because if it's
really, really good, it doesn't belong to
you, it doesn't belong to him. Do you
know who it belongs to? The Queen.
And if you go to Buckingham Palace
you'll see that it's stuffed full of old fossils.

Employment figures explained

1 person does 40 hours work

40 people do one hours work.

Conversation

I secretly recorded a conversation
I had with Corbyn on the 38 bus
on the day after the Miliband election.
I can now reveal he said,
'OK? Still writing poems?'
I said, 'Yes. You OK?'
He said, 'Yes.'

What a bastard.

The Mood

I love it
when an anchor person
sits in the studio in London,
looks up at a screen to someone in....
eg Paris
and says,
'What's the mood in France at the moment?'
What?!
Millions of people
with thousands of different moods
and they say
'What's the mood in France?'

Geometry

1. Create geometric myth of a 'centre' in politics.
2. Imply it's a natural, legitimate, decent place.
3. Promote its policies on war, inequality, privatisation as moderate.
4. Present criticism of these as extreme.
5. Repeat.

Mystery

Big mystery on the radio this morning:
how come there's a shortage of GPs?
er... they've taken up time-consuming hobbies?
er... they've gone into catering?

Tomorrow:
how come there are fewer teachers per pupil?
Researchers looking into evidence of teachers
taking up train-driving.

Cuts

Tory policy discussion:
Tory: 'We have saved the British economy
by cutting everything.'
Questioner: 'Er...there seem to be
a lot of cut-backs in the NHS, education, schools, benefits...'
Tory: 'We haven't cut anything.'

Questions

'The way we ask questions in English is with
who, why, where, how, when, what,
and we 'invert' modal and auxiliary verbs.'
'But what about with 'to be'?'
'No, not for a question.'
'What about, "To be or not to be that is the question"?'

Homeless

The homeless sleep under the bridge.
They make their beds on the pavement close to the wall.
The council put up a fence a metre from the wall.
The homeless leave.
Then the homeless come back.
They make their beds on the pavement close to the fence.
The homeless sleep under the bridge.

Theses

Just because we can break something down into bits, it doesn't mean that when we make that thing, we have to start with the bits.

If we say that we are made from what others do to us, we leave out the fact that we do things to others. If we say that we make others, we leave out that they make us.

We are born into a world that was made before we got there. We leave a world that we helped to make.

Everyone is someone else. You are someone else's someone else.

There is no such thing as a synonym because nothing is the same as anything else.

It's always today.

The dictionary definition of 'definition': what a dictionary defines is a definition.

We're all out of touch with something.

The older you get, the more the things that happened to you when you were young, matter.

Something not said is something not heard.

The media are much keener on hunting down imperfect individuals than exposing the atrocities of the powerful.

We are only fully contented when we have a league table for things. Am I eating Britain's most popular cake? Am I reading London's most important signpost? Do I weigh the world's most ideal weight?

Contradiction of our times: the more that internet sites compete with each other to display pix and vids, the less my not-so-broadband can cope with them.

Oversight and accountability are strict rules when governments want them to be strict rules. When they don't want them to be strict rules, the strict rules stop being strict rules.

Minorities matter. At some time or another, we are all minorities.

Policy

'Government policy'
isn't always policy.
You won't find anywhere
it's a 'policy' to close libraries.
They just close.
A mysterious hand locks the doors
and throws away the books,
and it never happens
by intention
because...
it's not written down that it's intended.

Bombing

The security wonks
move the bombers round the table.
Death sits under the table
counting.

Oscar

'And this year in the Oscars,
the winner for taking on multiple identities
and roles:
Death!
One moment, "collateral damage".
the next "unfortunate losses"!
Ladies and gentlemen,
I give you, Death.'

Interests

US foreign policy wonk on the radio
spoke about the forthcoming war with Iran,
assuring us that it would be
in self-defence
of American interests.
How come the US has 'interests'
thousands of miles from home?

And then, mysteriously,
these are therefore UK ones too!

Question

Who speaks?
Wrong question.
So what's the right question?
Who owns the platform?

Expert

You become the expert
because you're in power
and not:
you get the power
because you're the expert.

Invention

I've devised a shower-unit
that showers your brain.
If, say,
you've just heard Jacob Rees-Mogg
yet again
and you feel a bit mucky,
you just flush it all away
with my brain-shower.

Trade

Apparently,
when you sit opposite the Americans
negotiating a trade deal,
they tell you what the trade deal is.

Judeo-Christian

The New Right
say that they love
our 'Judeo-Christian culture'
and so in a stroke
wash away and clean up
hundreds of years of Christian
and post-Christian
persecution of Jews.

50 Years Since the Moon Landing

The good thing
about Evan Davies' interview
with Wernher Von Braun's daughter
is that he didn't spoil it
with impolite comments about
Wernher Von Braun's V2 rockets
landing on London
or slaves dying in the factories
that built them.

Jewish Leaders

I've got leaders?
Who gave them to me?
I don't remember asking for one.
I don't remember choosing one.

I'm worrying now:
how it is that I've managed
to do things
without knowing
who my leaders are.

How do I even think?

Kindertransport

Ah the Kindertransport!
Ideal for Tories to use
as an example of
Great British open-arms.

Other than that:
the doors were closed,
it was the grassroots
who brought them,
and the parents were kept out.

Gove

Gove looked
for an 'input-output' model
of assessing teachers;
first: narrow the 'output' of children
down to right/wrong answers
produced in tests,
as a way of assessing
the 'input' of teachers
teaching what the children would need
in order to come up with
right answers.

The subject chosen for these tests
was grammar
which meant reducing language
down to a way of describing
what we say and write
in such a way that it
can't explain why languages
vary or change.

That's because it's a description
of language that pretends
that language is a system
without humans being involved;
it often talks of language
or bits of language
'doing' things.
This ignores
the fact that
language is what
people do
when we speak, listen
write and read.
Language doesn't 'do' anything.
What happens is that
we do things with language.

The end result is that
Gove came up with a way of
testing teachers' effectiveness
at doing something useless.

Trump

Did Trump
abolish 'the elite'?

If Trump
didn't abolish the elite,
should we believe
that anyone from the Right
who says that
they are 'anti-elite'
is anti-elite?

Referendum

If the Referendum result was
'clear'
about what it was offering
by way of choice (in or out)
how come
there are so many variations of
what is 'out'?

If 'in' had won,
I suspect
that there would have been
some variations of
what is 'in'.

There is no binary solution
to how the UK aligns itself
to free trade blocs,
trading relations,
trade deals.
These are complex arrangements
between capitalists ('business')
overseen by governments.

Some capitalists
do better out of them
than others.

Where that leaves the rest of us
is out of our control.

I'm beginning to think
that doing things
in a binary way
may just possibly not be
the best way
of doing complicated things.

Train

Radio Armenia updated

Farage, May, Corbyn and a journalist are in a train that's stopped.
Farage says, 'Jump off the train'.
May says: 'I'm talking to the driver'.
Corbyn says: 'Actually you're talking to yourself'.
The journalist says, 'Close the curtains, and pretend we're moving.'

Analogy

I've decided
that the analogy for all this Brexit stuff
is the First World War:
a fight to the death between great powers
seeking domination,
which requires the cannon fodder of voters;
but in the end
(whichever way it goes)
will not benefit the surviving fodder
(while others will get rich on it.)

Dream

I have a dream that one day
I and others will walk hand in hand
to the polling station
and be able to vote
in an election
that is about
the NHS, education, benefits, wages, climate change...

BBC Breakfast

'Are you eating too many ultra-processed foods? They have been linked to overeating, early death and poor health.'

Dear BBC Breakfast
Can you please try another headline?
Manufacturers are making ultra-processed foods which have been linked to overeating, early death and poor health.

There is always the 'laudanum' argument.
In Victorian times,
you could go to a corner shop
and buy opium
to help your baby go to sleep.
It was called 'laudanum'.
Now we can't.

Surely Tory 'choice'
would require
that it should be available
so that we can decide
for ourselves.

Change

I joined the Independent Group.
Then I changed it to Change.
Then I changed.
Or it changed.
Or we changed.
So then I left
in order to be in the changed change party
which may be the alternative change.
Or the all-change.
Or the Spare Change Party.

Peterborough

One possible explanation
for Labour winning the Peterborough by-election
is that Peterborough is
jam packed
with around 10 thousand
middle-class Islington Corbynista cultists.

Trade Agreements

Before the referendum
a tiny elite
drew up trade agreements.
After the referendum
and after whatever arrangement
a tiny elite comes up with
a tiny elite will
draw up trade agreements.

Before the campaigning
for the Referendum
I didn't know anyone
who got off on
talking about trade agreements.

Now everyone does.

Our Interests

In the run-up to wars,
if you're a leading politician,
it's a good idea to talk about
'our interests' being 'in the region'
especially if it's 1000s of miles away;
then announce a violation
of these 'interests';

then imply or claim
that anyone sceptical of this
is a traitor.

Progress

Boris Johnson pioneered
a new election process:
in the future
all the candidates will hide
and we'll vote
on the basis of guessing
what they stand for.

The Tory Party Leadership Campaign

Chefs competing to produce meals
which we never get to eat.

Job

It's not the job
of leading politicians
to be competent.
It's their job to look competent.

The job of the media
is not to question politicians' competence.
It's to support them
in their attempt to look competent.

Cheaper

Wouldn't it be quicker
and cheaper
to abolish elections
and just let the Head of Eton
choose
who should be prime minister?

Defence

Love Boris Johnson's great-grandfather defence:
how can I be Islamophobic
when my great grandfather was a Muslim?

On that basis Nazis' great-grandchildren
must be Nazis.

Actually, I can't be sexist:
my great grandmother was a woman.

TV

Some hours can go by
in a haze of interviewers
talking to commentators
talking about the interview
they commentated on
earlier.

Charm

Today
I'm panicking:
commentators keep
describing Boris Johnson
as 'charming'
and I don't feel charmed.
What's wrong with me?

Spectacle

The election of a new Tory leader
was a display, an exhibition, a spectacle,
in which we had no say.
It was produced, directed and designed
for the benefit of the Tory Party
so that it could stay in power.

To make sure
that the spectacle ran smoothly
the media
were willing stage hands.

The meaning of all this
was less in what was actually said
but much more in that the display
was for a while constant
coming at us from all sides
day after day after day.

It was an illusion that we were
being included
being considered
when in fact it was just
a matter of being pushed into our faces.

Mobile

Justine Greening
is going to do social mobility.
She thinks some people
have been left behind
over the last few years.
She won't be abolishing private schools,
tax havens
or inherited wealth.
Justine Greening
is not doing social mobility.

Talking about social mobility
is a way of sounding fair
while keeping everything unfair.

Social Mobility (reg trade mark)
is a board game most people can't win.
But if you don't win it,
it's your fault.

Clerihews

JS Bach
to his wife, said 'Ach!
You think your Kapellmeister
is just a shyster?'

Mark Twain
was on a train
when he said to his employer:
'I'm gonna write *Tom Sawyer*.'
When he'd packed it in.
He wrote *Huckleberry Finn*.

Aesop's Fables
often turn tables
on whichever beast
thinks the least.

Mary Shelley
didn't have a telly.
She did fine
inventing Frankenstein.

I've got a dog called Marx
whose skill is he barks...
(when I feed him pesto)
...*The Communist Manifesto*.

Madame Curie
(imagine her fury)
who they said's beyond the pale
for being Polish and female.

Gustave Flaubert
fell for his au pair.
It was meant to be ethereal
but it became venereal.

George Frederick Handel
loved to dandle
his fingers in the Thames
from which the *Water Music* stems.

On Sir Richard Francis Burton
we should pull down the curtain,
and seek an official pardon
for *The Perfumed Garden*.

Walter de la Mare
had cash to spare.
We should give thanks
that he worked in banks.

Ringo Starr
could have gone far.
Probs would have had another hit
but the Beatles split.

Geoffrey Chaucer
in a flying saucer
wrote a series of emails
called The Planetary Tales

Samuel Taylor Coleridge
was rather fond of foliage.
He found the world much barrener
when he met the Ancient Mariner.

Edgar Allan Poe
had nightmares, so
produced many a word
about being interred.

Isambard Kingdom Brunel
constructed 'un tunnel'
between Rotherhithe and Wapping,
so now there's no stopping.

William Shakespeare
wrote *King Lear*.
People who are mistaken
think it was Francis Bacon.

Wenger (Arsène)
had the air of a parson.
If something was messy, he'd want to clean it.
If something was dodgy, he hadn't seen it.

Bertrand Russell
had a bit of a tussle
with tan and cosine
and Lady Ottoline.

Sir Alexander Fleming
drew conclusions stemming
from some bread that was old
and covered in mould.

Noel Coward
in the mid-century, flowered.
With encounters, he was the chief
but they weren't always Brief.

Bishop Berkeley
put it starkly:
just believe
what you perceive.

Emile Zola
spun life's tombola:
'Win or lose,
I say, 'J'accuse'.'

What would Herbert Marcuse
make of the accuser
who said 'cultural marxist' but knew
he just meant 'Jew'?

George Bernard Shaw
in a mirror saw:
the world's greatest writer of plays,
(He did this most days).

Michelangelo Buonarotti
felt a bit grotty.
He got over this feeling,
and painted the Sistine ceiling.

Orson Welles
made a movie that tells
how a citizen called Kane
was a bit of a pain.

Sigmund Freud
was overjoyed:
he heard we're obsessed
with the return of the repressed.

John Donne
resented the sun.
He wanted to be
his wife's flea.

Emily Bronte
liked the full monty:
obsession and passion
and outdoor fashion.

Robert Zimmerman
sang the song 'Sinner Man'.
When he played the harmonica
he sounded laconic-er.

Alfred, Lord Tennyson
often made mention
in tones overawed
of a woman called Maud.

Sir Thomas Malory
used up many a calorie
writing about Arthur (his Morte)
and loads more about the court.

William Morris
would have hated Boris
he preferred a revolutionary meetin'
to former pupils of Eton.

Bertolt Brecht
is the one for an echt
incarnation
of alienation.

Jonathan Swift
had the gift
of being ironic
about the plague (Bubonic)

WE Johns'
creations
focussed on Biggles:
not many giggles.

Jacques Brel
experienced hell.
The devil said, (believe me)
'Ne *me quitte pas*' ('Don't leave me').

Umberto Eco
was fond of Prosecco
The result was eerie:
he mixed fiction with theory.

Roland Barthes
made a great start.
In the end he was beat
when he crossed the street.

Kafka (Franz)
took the stance:
life doesn't start well
and the rest is hell.

Jean-Paul Sartre
didn't like Chartres:
the path he trod
avoided God.

Leon Trotsky
wrote a lotsky.
He often made refsky
to Alexander Nevsky.

Garibaldi
shopped at Aldi
he bought biscuits – no lies –
that were stuffed full of flies.

Jacob Rees-Mogg
was totally agog
if not craven
about a new tax-haven.

Marcel Pagnol
owned an old *bagnole*
He needed cash to restore it
so he wrote *Jean de Florette*.

Count Leo Tolstoy
adored the Bolshoi.
Maybe he saw a ballerina
called Anna Karenina.

Henry Moore
was very sure
how to knock
a piece of rock.

'Philip Roth
was obsessed with a moth.'
'No! that was Nabokov.
So knock it off.'

Thomas Hardy
got a bit mardy
when people were rude
about Tess and Jude.

Charles Dickens
wrote about slim pickins:
most famously for him
about Tiny Tim.

Rudyard Kipling
found identity crippling,
It's a matter of opinion
as to whether he was Indian.

The words of Kenneth Grahame
is in how you say'em.
The decline of Toad Hall
is not a disaster for us all.
The collapse of the aristocracy
is not a crisis for democracy.

Pete Seeger
was often eager
to assemble throngs
to sing songs.

Céline
was rather mean.
He was thought to be artsy.
He was in fact a Nazi.

Leonard Cohen
died still owin'
Suzanne
her kaftan.

Ted Hughes
would often refuse
to take the path
of talking about Plath.

Did Farrokh Bulsara
play Connemara?
You know who could say?
Brian May.

Jean-Jacques Rousseau
had nothing to do so
he wrote a good deal
about Émile.

Lorraine Kelly
read Machiavelli:
'I'm someone who acts
so I pay less tax.'

The Coalition
of its own volition
chose to fress*
the NHS.

Debbie Harry
didn't marry.
And 'One Way or Another'
is not about her brother.

The Duchess of Windsor
always begins her
day with nothing purer
than a thought of the Führer.

Margaret Thatcher:
hated manufacture,
was inclined to hector,
and loved the financial sector.

Igor Stravinsky
worked with Nijinsky.
At the start it was quiet.
It ended with a riot.

Albert Camus
said, 'I'm you.
It's about control.
And I'm in goal.'

Boris Johnson proves the rule
that no MP can be a fool
Any of us could easily forget
we owned a house in Somerset.

Walter Scott
was not
into rationalism.
He invented nationalism.

Ian McMillan
is Barnsley's Bob Dylan,
or (more accurately) the Garfield
of Darfield.

John Milton
stayed at the Hilton.
Not that John Milton.
Some other John Milton.

Roger Scruton
visited Luton
Wrote home: 'Am horrified to see
there are people here who don't look like me.'